BURNS

BURNS

FIRST EDITION

IKPE O. VITALIS, PHD, FMLSCN, FCAI

DEPARTMENT OF BIOCHEMISTRY

CARITAS UNIVERSITY

AMORJI-NIKE

ENUGU, ENUGU STATE

NIGERIA

PARTRIDGE

A Penguin Random House Company

To order additional copies of this book, contact
Toll Free 0800 990 914 (South Africa)
+44 20 3014 3997 (outside South Africa)
orders.africa@partridgepublishing.com

www.partridgepublishing.com/africa

Contents

1.0   CHAPTER ONE

INTRODUCTION

B urns are injuries sustained from contact with heat energies, chemical agents or their combined effect and are classified as chemical, electrical, fire or radiation. External and internal structures can be affected depending on the intensity and duration of exposure since a burn wound remain a function of the heat load, the duration of contact and the conductibility of the affected tissue. Inhaled smoke causes respiratory distress that may be life threatening.

Burns occur mainly due to negligence, carelessness, civilization, family indulgence and other risky practices that are avoidable with destruction of houses, markets, offices, institutions, oil installations and farmlands. Survival possibility for badly burned victims is doubtful but those that escape death live with scars, disfigurement or disability.

Burn incidences are more frequent during summer or harmatan season due to the dry nature of the atmosphere and the environment. The elderly and the very young are mostly at risk while factory workers face challenges from flammable, hazardous and electrical materials.

Management of burn victims is always an intensive practice by a team of the medical profession with specialized training. The objective of treatment is to resuscitate, stabilize and sustain the victim. Burn casualties usually stay longer on admission than other patients attracting bills that may require 'donations' to pay.

Burns constitute public health hazard and global tragedies. Lost lives are irreplaceable and some properties irretrievable. Monetary losses are only estimated not exactly quantified by individuals, corporate bodies or government. Concerted efforts are recommended as remedies but preventive measures are gold standards.

2.0   CHAPTER TWO

TYPES OF BURNS

2.1 BURNS FROM FIRES

Burns from fires or flame burns occur frequently and the extent of structural injury depends upon several factors including the intensity of heat tissue affected. The conductance of the tissues affected determines the rate of dissipation or absorption of heat. Operating factors are the peripheral circulation, water content of the tissue, thickness of the skin and its pigmentation, of the presence or absence of external insulting substances such as hair and skin oil. Of these factors the most important in determining the degree of injury is the peripheral circulation. The rate of blood flow through the heat-exposed tissues can be altered rapidly. This mechanism is of major importance in determining the amount of cellular destruction associated with the transfer of heat to the tissue. Flame burns occur through ignition of clothing from unguarded gas and electric fires, open coal fires, explosion of paraffin and petrol ignited bonfires, car fires following road traffic accidents, car radiator-related burns, stored petrol in homes, and smoking in petrol stations and generators.

Thermal injury due to hot air is rare. For such a burn to occur, the air stream from some form of artificial heat source such as a hair drier or fan heater has to be concentrated on a localized area of the victim's body. The source has to be close enough to the skin to raise the temperature sufficiently to cause injury. During an epileptic fit, victims are susceptible since they cannot remove themselves from the source.

Hot metal burns are not rare. Burns due to molten metal occur in men working in foundries. In the typical injury, the molten metal is splashed or spilled onto the legs and some of it may run down inside the boots, causing burns of the feet. Home radiators and hot pipe are other sources of burn injury and may result in full skin structural burn. The elderly along with children and people with handicaps are at increased risk in the normal domestic environment..

Burns occur by the use of cigarettes and oxygen therapy especially with admitted patients. Most scald injuries are considered to be home accidents involving tea, coffee or boiling water. Although simple precautions could virtually eliminate this major cause of burn mobidity, there is little evidence that the incidence of tap water scald burns has decreased significantly. It seems clear that the young, the elderly and black skinned people are the groups at highest risk for tape water scald burn injury, whether fatal or not.

Injuries due to accidental contact with steam are occasionally encountered. This type of injury can result in serious work-related disability. Blistering and slough of the bronchial mucosa are common. The severity of injury depends on the temperature of the steam, duration of exposure, distance of the victim from the source of the steam and the ability of the worker to escape the steam.

Elderly people are particularly at risk of accidents in the home. Domestic hot water burns are a common and preventable cause of injury. Elderly people tend to have reduced mobility that result in slower reaction times, making them more susceptible to scalds. The elderly people suffer increased mortality and morbidity and a reduction in independence, even after minor burns. Partial thickness burns in adults can occur in thirty seconds at a temperature of 55°C, five seconds at 60°C and one second at 65°C. Elderly people have thin skin and poor microcirculation, hence heat is removed from burned tissues rather slowly when compared to younger adults, often resulting in scalds that are more serious. Hot water should be stored at a temperature of greater than 60°C to avoid infection by organisms that thrive at low temperatures. In facilities with body immersion, showers and baths there should be thermostatic mixers, located in the hot water system before the tap, which cut off hot water in less than one second at temperature above 45°C.

The mechanism of burn injury is one of the most important determinants of the severity of tissue damage by burn. Although only hot liquid burn is regarded as scalds, the burn caused by liquids with higher boiling point such as certain oils, can cause significantly deep burn injury. The other important determinant of the severity is the contact period as in case of immersion scalds.

Earthquake related burns occurs along with wide-scale destruction of buildings and infrastructures. Disruption of gas, fuel pipes, tankers and multiple home fires lead to fire related death.

Quick freeze injury or frost bite following exposure to cold liquids and gases at extremely low temperature is an occupational hazard. This occurs with liquid helium at -273°C and vapour at -269°C to -180°C. Cold injuries due to accidental leakage of nitrous oxide, frostbite following recreational use of nitrous oxide and gas are possibilities, others are injuries caused by the use of liquid nitrogen, liquid propane, quick freeze injury by spray containing propane and butane as propellants and frostbite injury to the oral cavity with inhaled aerosolized propane propellant.

The widespread use of pressurized aerosol cans and subsequent disposal in domestic and public burnable trash is a source of superficial flash burn. A prominent warning of the fire and explosive hazard of these cans on the front side of the can as well as increased public awareness of the potential dangers of these containers, would be helpful in decreasing the incidence of these injuries.

Burns can also be sustained by standing or walking barefoot on the street especially during the summer months when the ground temperature is estimated to be in the range of 50-60C. Burn injuries that involve the sole of the foot are usually caused by standing or stepping on hot materials such as ash, beach fires, hot desert sand or by immersion in hot water.

2.2 BURNS FROM ELECTRICITY

Electrical injuries result from the heat produced by the flow of electrical current through the resistance of body tissues. Factors of primary importance in determining the effect of the passage of an electric current through the human body include the type of circuit, voltage, amperage, resistance of the tissues involved, the path of the current through the body and duration of contact with the current. The main reason for considering these injuries as a distinct from the more common thermal burn is the volume of tissue that is affected in high voltage electrical injuries. Electrical injury may be classified according to the intensity of the voltage and is considered as high tension (>1000v) and low tension (< 1000 v). The nature of the current is also an important aspect to be observed, since alternating current to the circuit causes more devastating effects compared to direct current. In the latter, muscle spasm ejects the victim away from the power source and interrupts the thermal injury. The pattern of contact with the electrical source classifies the burn as direct, where the sites of entry and exit of the current can be easily found at inspection; as arc when the body approaches the energy radius closing the circuit, or as flash burn when it occurs by instantaneous ignition of clothing or environmental objects due to electrical current. By mechanism, electrical current enters the body at the point of contact, travels along planes and structures of low resistance and exits through the earth contact. Only the contact points initially produce visible skin injury. Factors, which influence the amount of tissue damage, include Voltage – high tension voltages ionize the air particles and may arc across several meters, Amperage (current) determines the heat generated, and Resistance - in ascending order of resistance (least resistance first) blood vessels, nerve, muscle, skin, tendon, fat, bone provide a pathway for passage of the current. Thrombosis of blood vessels may result in ischaemic or venous gangrene of tissue supplied by those vessels, some distance from the burn injury. Dry skin offers a resistance of about 1 million ohms, whereas moist skin only 35,000 ohms. Skin immersed in water has a resistance of 1000 ohms. Tissue damage is principally determined by voltage. Nerves and blood vessels are good to excellent conductors, muscle less so, and skin and bone are particularly resistant to the passage of electricity. Although resistance is important, voltage is exponentially more important (the square of the voltage). Low-voltage injuries can be fatal because of the alteration of the cardiac cycle by passage by the current; higher-voltage injuries can cause concomitant tissue damage.

Physiologically, burning by contact with electrical current, which passes through the body, has effects upon the heart, brain, abdominal cavity, muscle, or blood vessels and nerves. In addition it destroys the skin, which comes into contact with the electrical source. Considerably greater quantities of tissue may be destroyed beneath intact skin than is superficially apparent. Alternating current produces greater damage than direct current. Most injuries are caused by the low-tension 240-volt alternating domestic supply. Less common injuries occur from high-tension electrical supply such as from railway overhead conductors (25 000 volts AC), conductor rails (750 volts DC) or from National Grid electrical cabling (400 000 – 30 000 volts AC). In high-tension injuries, the current passes through the skin up to the limb, causing extensive necrosis of muscles, nerves and vessels

Low-tension burns are flash burns, electric fire filament or electric bar burns and contact with live wire. Flash burns are caused by momentary exposure of the skin, usually the face and hands, to flash heat without actual contact of the skin to the electrical conductor. Electric fire filament or electric bar burns are of the hands and affects the entire structures. The main injuring agent is the heat rather than the electrical current. With children, bone growth is reduced, due to scar formation inhibiting bone growth. The victim in contact with live wire requires to be disconnected either by turning off the power source or using a non-conductor material. The contact point burn may be only one or two centimeters in diameter, but because of titanic contraction the victim may be unable to disconnect himself from the source. Hands and mouth (babies chewing wires) are frequent sites. The point of exit of the current from the body is the soles of the feet.

Electric arc burns are high-tension arcs and cause injury through intense heat or flash. The current may earth itself through the victim in contact with the ground, may leap to another nearby object or return to the source. For high-tension injuries physical contact with the wire or cable is not necessary, since the victim may act as conductor in an electrical arc. Unconsciousness and death often occur with electrical injuries. Shock occurs only in severe high-tension injuries and in association with severe muscle damage.

Electrical injuries sustained by contact between heavy machinery and high-tension power lines are an occasional cause of work related injury. Workmen touching the construction equipment or cables attached to the machinery while standing on the ground may suffer electrocution.

The spectrum of electrical injuries is complex, has multiple variables and is sometimes unpredictable. The mechanism is unique and the destructive potential of electrical energy is great. The source of electricity can vary from lightening to batteries and telephone wires. Most electrical injuries appear to arise from ignorance, curiosity or carelessness. The electricity board stipulates that the minimum distance between high-tension lines and telephone lines should not be less than 25 meters but this is not adhered to. The solution to this problem is to cover the telephone wire with non-conducting material like heavy Teflon in the areas where they cross electric cables.

Railway and subway-associated electrical injury is rare and typically involves high voltage (> 20000v). Not all rail systems utilize such high voltage. Among subway workers the mechanism of rail contact was unintentional by a tool, a hand or by falling. Among non-occupational victims, injuries involved suicide attempts, unintentional falls or risk-taking behaviour. Most of these injuries are mechanical and occur when an individual or a moving vehicle is hit by a train. High voltage (25 000 V, alternating current) arc injury due to overhead railway cables also occur. Household electrocutions (120 – 220v) and high-tension electrocutios (> 1000 V) are common.

A bolt of lightning is another source of burns but very uncommon. Dying instantly through lightning-induced cardiac arrest is possible. There are variations in current type, voltage and amperage between lightning and supplied electricity, and the difference in contact time with the electrical current in the different accident situations causes different damage to the tissue and the body. There are three major ways to get struck by lightning. A direct hit to the head will almost kill the victim instantly. The electrical energy of a ground or stride current originating from an adjacent object, like a tree, or a flash over injury does not usually exceed the breakdown strength of the skin and can skate over the person to dissipate on the ground. Contact strikes will occur when a person is in touch with an object being hit. Lightning can be seen as a very long spark produced by a transient high-current discharge to the earth. The thermal energy can turn superficial moisture such as sweat, saliva, tears or rainwater into steam, which explains the frequent affliction of exposed mucous membranes. For flashover injuries, the energy rarely exceeds the breakdown strength of the skin as the body's primary resistor to electrical flow. The mechanism is due to shattered blood components from dermal capillaries, electron showers eliciting an inflammatory reaction or a result of the current following lines of skin moisture.

2.3 BURNS FROM CHEMICALS

Different chemicals are used in industrial processes and laboratories. Safety precautions have dramatically reduced the incidence of burn accidents from these sources. However, domestic accidents continue to occur with unacceptable frequency, and burns deliberately inflicted in time of war from gas, toxic chemicals, incendiary bombs, criminal assault and conflagrations resulting from explosions constitute a significant proportion of the burn casualties. Some agents (e.g chromic and formic acids, phenol and organic chemicals) are absorbed through the skin and alter the liver and kidney in addition to the local effects on the skin. The majority of chemical agents produce skin destruction through chemical reactions which Include coagulation of protein by reduction, corrosion, oxidation, formation of salts, poisoning of protoplasm and desiccation. Acids promote collagen denaturation and subsequent degradations. Heat production is often a by-product of the chemical reactions with tissues and may worsen the injury.

ACIDS: Hydrochloric and Nitric acids produce injuries by local coagulation of skin, subcutaneous tissue and thrombosis of vessels. Also absorbed into the circulation to cause acidosis (rapid respiration) or renal failure (anuria or high volume of urine with inability to concentrate the urine above specific gravity of 1.010). Hydrofluoric acid is extensively used in chemical plants in the production of high-octane fuel. To a lesser extent it is used in glass etching, electroplating and production of insecticides and refrigerants and as a cleaning agent for toilet walls and surrounds and granite surfaces. H_2SO_4, Chromic acid, tannic acid, formic acid and picric acid produce burn injuries. Chromic acid may be absorbed to produce liver and renal damage. Ingestion causes peripheral vascular collapse, cramps, coma and glycosuria. Magnesium oxide, limewater and soap are antidotes. Deep dermal burns usually result from contact with a source of heat, electricity or chemicals.

ALKALIS: Some examples are sodium hydroxide, potassium hydroxide, ammonium hydroxide and calcium oxide (lime). These cause local dehydration of tissue, destruction of proteins and fat and absorption to cause metabolic alkalosis (muscle twitching and spasm). Sodium hypochlorite is widely in bleaches, disinfectants and deodorizers. The free chlorine coagulates proteins and swallowing leads to damage of oesophageal structures, vomiting, confusion and coma. Metallic sodium, potassium and lithium explode and ignite on contact with water.

Phosphorus burns in contact with air and is caused by incendiary bombs. Particles of elemental phosphorus are liable to be driven into the tissues and will continue to cause damage until washed or picked out. When the large pieces have been removed residual small ones can be identified by darkening the room and observing phosphorescence. Alternatively, running small amounts of copper sulphate suspension onto the skin converts the phosphorus into copper phosphate, which can easily be seen as black particles. With delayed or no treatment, phosphorus absorption leads to liver and kidney damage.

Organic chemicals include petrol, phenol (carbolic acid), trilene and cresol (lysol). They are absorbed through the skin and may cause cardiac, respiratory, renal and liver failure, convulsions and coma. Phenol penetrates deeply into the skin and unless the chemical is removed quickly enough, it may be absorbed to give systemic and local effects. The phenol will continue to penetrate deeply causing further damage and enough may be absorbed to cause toxic effects of which kidney damage is the most important. Phenol burns and intoxications are life-threatening injuries. Phenol is an aromatic hydrocarbon derived from coal tar.

Asphalt workers may splash hot bitumen onto the skin. This rapidly sets into a hard wad, which adheres to the wounds. Bitumen is a general term for petroleum-derived substances ranging from so-called mineral tars, to asphalt. Asphat (Asphaltum) is a semi-solid mixture of several hydrocarbons probably formed by the evaporation of the lighter or more volatile constituents. It is amorphous, of low specific gravity with a black or brownish black colour and pitchy luster. At room temperature it is solid becoming molten and spreadable when heated to 93°C and over. Roofing tars and asphalts are usually heated to temperature of 232°C to achieve desirable viscosities (e.g. for spraying), whereas lower temperatures are required for the manageable form to pave roads. Bitumen burns may involve the critical areas – the face, orbits, hands and feet. Most accidents occur through falls and spillage and are independent of the experience of the worker. Prevention depends on continuing worker education, safe work practices and the development of accident safe equipment. Simple and basic preventive measures such as carrying hot air in containers with long gloves and long sleeve shirts, wearing goggles to protect the eyes and wearing heavy pants and boots might reduce the incidence and degree of burns.

Potassium permanganate is also a source of burns. It is used in disinfectant bleaches and deodorizers. It stains the tissues purple and oxidizes to destruction. Another type of burn is the cooking fat burn and increasingly common is the chip pan fat burn. When the fat ignites in the pan, instead of turning off the gas or electricity and capping the pan with a pot lid or plate to exclude air, the anxious cook lifts the pan off the oven and runs towards the door, the flames streaming backwards onto her arm, spilling ignited fat onto her legs. Swallowing of domestic bleaches by children is the main cause of oesophageal burns. Exposure to inhaled gases (e.g. ammonia, methyllisocyanate) produces inflammatory reaction. Ammonia has a potential to cause damage due to its toxic, alkaline chemical nature. In addition, it may cause a frostbite injury due to its cooling effect. Ammonia is a colourless gas with a strong pungent and irritating odour. It is highly water soluble about 1300 volumes can dissolve in one volume of water forming ammonium hydroxide, which is highly caustic. Ammonia due to its high water solubility is known to affect the respiratory system, the eyes and the skin. The solubility of a gas in aqueous environment governs the depth to which a gas will affect the respiratory tract. Gases such as nitrogen dioxide and phosgene are deep lung irritants. However, when inhaled over a long period of time at a high concentration, it can severely affect the lower respiratory tract. Destruction of mucous glands, smooth muscle and cartilage occur. Cold thermal injury from exposure to pressurized liquid nitrous oxide, liquid nitrogen, liquid propane and liquid helium are additional sources. Employees need to be educated with respect to health hazards as well as protective measures including gas tight chemical goggles, self contained breathing apparatus, rubber boots, gloves and complete gas suits in case of gas leaks.

Alkali burns of the eye are more severe than acid burns because of the rapid penetration through the cornea and anterior chamber, combining with cell membrane lipids thereby resulting in disruption of the cells. Chemical burns of the eye vary greatly from the points of view of severity and prognosis. Mild burns are painful but do not reduce vision significantly nor remove the victim from the work force for a substantial period of time. Alkali burns are the most serious chemical injuries of the eye. Substances such as lime (CaO) cause more damage than acids because of their rapid penetration through the cornea and the anterior chamber. Damage is related to the pH, the higher the pH the greater the damage to the eye, with the most significant injury occurring around pH 11 – 11.5. Chemical burns are classified as toxic, acid and alkali. The severity of any burn is dependent on the concentration of the causative agent, the duration of exposure and the pH of the solution. A toxic chemical injury may be one with inherent properties inimical to cell membranes. Its penetration may be rapid and damage is evident, or if poor induce changes limited to the epithelium. Weak acids do not penetrate biological tissues very well. The hydrogen ion precipitates protein on contact. Alkalis and very strong acids penetrate rapidly to cloud plasma membranes and denature collagen.

Chemical burn due to contact with soda lime on the playground is a potential hazard for football players. The burn is of the alkali type and is rarely reported in industry, although it remains a threat for cement and other workers in the chemical industry. Some footballers have had burning sensation of their genitalia and thigh. The mechanism of the lesion is that the soda lime powder used for line marking in playgrounds is made of calcium oxide that is not corrosive by itself. The compound is alkaline and its admixture with water results in a thermic reaction.

The active compound calcium hydroxide is alkaline with a pH of between 12.4 and 12.7 and produces heat.

Industrial burn injuries are not rare, but chemical injuries are unusual and often poorly understood in terms of the relative contributions of heat and chemical damage.. Zinc oxide is acid and alkali soluble and only sparingly water-soluble. Its boiling point (907°C) and fusion point (419°C) at high temperatures and in the presence of water it carries a significant explosion rate. The burns are mostly due to the heat content of the zinc oxide particles following the explosion and embedding in the skin. Zinc oxide is virtually insoluble in water and is only a very weak base. Molten zinc becomes zinc oxide (vapour) in an atmosphere temperature and changes to solid at a low temperature. Under these circumstances hot particles of zinc oxide can be blasted into the skin. Such burns should be preventable by the provision of appropriate protective shielding and observance of safety regulations by staff. Additional care and education in the special chemicals industry is required to produce a further reduction in the incidence of these potentially serious injuries.

Burns can result from the application of hair removal cream on thin areas such as the lower abdomen, groins and inner thighs. Hair removal lotions or creams are used to remove unwanted body hairs of legs, under-arms and private areas. Whereas shaving cuts off the hair, cream gently melt the hair leaving a soft tip from where hair regrows. It does not normally cause any major problem on normal skin except minor skin irritation and adverse reaction when it is used on skin with moles, spots, broken or sun damage. Hair removal cream is a chemical depilatory gel cream which dissolves the hair leaving a soft tip under the surface of the skin. Although hair removal creams vary between different manufacturers, they use the chemical thioglycolate mixed with sodium hydroxide or calcium hydroxide to melt the hair away. Thioglycolate disrupts disulphide bonds, which are chemical bonds that hold skin and hair cells together. Thioglycolate is more effective on disulphide bonds that contain cystine. The major side effect of a depilatory is skin irritation because the chemical can melt away skin cells.

Manufacturers advice the removal of the cream and to rinse thoroughly with water if there is irritation and burning. There is also suggestion for patch test (product information leaflet) to see the skin reaction if using first time on a new body part and asked not to use on blemished, broken, irritated or sunburnt skin. Pulling off the pubic hair breaches the surface of skin for the cream to cause chemical burns.

Chemical hair care products exposed to flame cause burns of the face, scalp, ear, back and neck. The sources of ignition are cigarette lighters, stove pilot lights, gas stove burners or matches in an enclosed space. Other risky practices include lighting a cigarette in the car or in a telephone booth, bending over a gas range while cooking, burning a string from an article of clothing, lighting a pilot light in the oven, and lighting a cigarette from an electric range.

Vesicant burns are due to chemical warfare agents and include the mustards, the arsines (lewisite) and the halogenated oximes (Phosgene oxime). The most widely used of these agents is sulphur mustard. The other important vesicant agent is lewisite, its effects are similar to mustard but has a more profound systemic toxicity. Phosgene oxime produces blisters, but unlike sulphur mustard, the irritation caused by exposure is almost immediate. Sulphur mustard and lewisite produce blisters in man on the area directly exposed to the agent.

However, ocular irritation can occur at much lower concentrations of vapour than would cause skin blistering. Systemic effects, including bone marrow depression occur if the absorbed dose is sufficiently high. The main aim of vesicant agents is incapacitation for a long time with casualties of a non-fatal but possibly long term nature. Sulphur mustard [bis (2-chloroethyl) sulphide was first synthesized around 1822. The pure form of sulphur mustard is designated HD (distilled mustard), but weapons grade may contain 10-40% impurities.

Lewisite (2-chlorovinyl-dichlorarsine) is the best known of the arsines and was first produced in its pure form in 1918. Phosgene oxime is a halogenated oxime. Vesicant burns may arise either from exposure to the vapour or to the liquid. The burn caused by blister agent behaves in much the same way as thermal burn, but does not continue to penetrate like an acid burn. However, it is much slower to heal, taking about twice the time of a comparable thermal burn. Two factors are involved. Firstly, the epidermal cells at the edge of the burn may be damaged and not proliferate at the normal rate. Secondly, the altered collagen may not provide a satisfactory matrix over which the epidermal cells can spread. Characteristically, the healing area loses its pigment, whilst the area of damaged cells surrounding the original lesion becomes hyper pigmented.

2.4 BURNS FROM RADIATION

This is divided into radiation burns and burns due to nuclear explosions. Radiation burns arise from inadvertent escape of nuclear fuels, accidents during radiotherapy or deliberate use of destructive weapons. The electromagnetic spectrum includes radiowaves, infrared, visible light, ultraviolet, X-rays and gamma rays in decreasing order of wavelength and all travel at the same speed. The ability to penetrate living tissue depends on the wavelength and wave frequency. Thus, radiowaves and visible light penetrate little or not at all while x-rays and gamma rays penetrate deeply. Repeated exposure leads to tissue damage. Onset of apparent effects of injury is shortest with long wavelength radiation, i.e. infrared 'sunburn' and the longest with gamma rays. Damage at cellular level affects mitosis, enzyme systems and metabolism. Blistering, erythema and swelling of the skin is the minimal reaction, which either returns to normal with little permanent change or progresses to vessel damage. Healing is slow and may result in scar formation.

Radiation burns are due to excessive doses during radiotherapy, radiodiagnosis, radioactive materials and weapons or to accidents involving nuclear energy apparatus. In the acute stage, within one or two days of the irradiation, the affected area becomes red and swollen and may blister. In most instances, the burn is essentially superficial and heals slowly over course of a few months. In other instances where the initial damage is less acute, the early changes may be mild and transient but chronic changes appear months or years later. In the most severe forms of radiation damage, destruction may be so severe that healing never occurs.

Many burns following nuclear explosions are due to the intense heat-flash and others from the conflagration started by the heat. A minority is likely to be due to the radiation itself. Acute burns due to nuclear radiations (neutrons, gamma-rays and x-rays) rarely occur because anyone close to the center of the explosion to receive a sufficient skin dose to cause a burn receives a fatal dose of irradiation or may be killed by heat.

Burns from sunbeds and sunlamps occur if recommended exposure times are exceeded. Faulty equipment may also injure through excessive dosage. Cutaneous burn injury and ocular (corneal and/or retinal) injury are the commonest acute complications following the use of sun tanning devices. In modern suntanning devices most UVB and UVC light (the spectra known to be most harmful in causing skin cancers is filtered out. The remaining UVA may cause skin injury, including burns, if either the recommended tanning times are exceeded or if the tannee has an innate or medication-potentiated skin sensitivity. The need for fail-safe mechanisms in sunbeds and sunlamps to detect filter slippage or absence which inactivates the power supply is obvious.

2.5 BURNS FROM INHALATION

These may result from smoke from unwanted and uncontrolled fires, exposure to cigarette smoke, smog, chemical fumes or the repetitive exposures which occur in firefighters. Smoke refers to the airborne products of incomplete thermal degradation of material. Smoke inhalation injury constitutes an injury to the proximal airway or pulmonary parenchyma, severe enough to result in detectable clinical consequences. Thermal decomposition of material may be accompanied by flames (combustion) or be without flame. Smoke moves easily in response to winds and drafts so that injury can occur at sites remote from the fire. The hypoxia resulting from carbon monoxide and cyanide compound in smoke interferes with correct perceptions and reduces physical capacities which are the reasons for the inappropriate responses and feeble escape efforts often seen. Smoke reduces visibility and is a powerful eye irritant thus interfering with both escape and rescue. Many smoke victims do not survive long enough to enter the health care system. Conditions of acute alcoholism, coronary artery disease, pre-existing illness, cyanide, heavy metals and other toxins contribute to death. The diagnosis of inhalation burn is occasionally obvious, occasionally difficult. The diagnostic procedures of smoke inhalations include history, physical examination, laboratory evaluation and chest imaging.

Red cell destruction in burned skin reduces oxygen carriage by haemoglobin compounding the problems; there is an increased oxygen requirement at cellular level. Hot dry air cools rapidly and thus the internal damage from this is usually confined to the respiratory tract. The lower respiratory tract is more frequently affected by steam or explosion releasing hot or toxic gas. Since water has a high heat carrying capacity, it may still be hot when it reaches the alveoli. This causes inflammable exudates and thickening of the alveolar walls reducing gaseous exchange. Thermal injury may lead to eye damage or a deficiency of surfactant. This substance lowers the surface tension of the walls of the alveoli which helps to maintain their patency. A deficiency of surfactant leads to collapse of alveoli. An explosion in a confined space may cause pressure effects on the lung tissue..

Carbon monoxide is produced by the incomplete combustion of carbon and occurs when a fire has developed in a confined space. Carbon monoxide has no taste or smell and when inhaled, combines with haemoglobin to form carboxyhaemoglobin. Carbon monoxide has an affinity for haemoglobin which is 200 times that of oxygen and so displaces oxygen carried in the blood by haemoglobin. This leads to tissue hypoxia. Victims with carbon monoxide poisoning are cherry pink in colour, although they are anoxic. Carboxyhaemoglobin levels of 5% are commonly found in burned patients on admission. Unconsciousness develops at a carboxyhaemoglobin level of 30%. Hypoxia may occur due to depletion of the available oxygen in the air when combustion takes place in a confined space or when the inhalation of smoke displaces oxygen from the inspired air. Inhaled smoke or chemical irritants may produce severe pulmonary oedema and bronchospasm or may interfere with capillary permeability. The direct toxic effects of gases produced when modern materials ignite may also be lethal. Polyurethane foam widely used as a filter in modern furniture gives off smoke containing isocyanates which break down to hydrogen cyanate, carbon monoxide and ammonia. At 1000°C, hydrogen cyanide is produced. Death from cyanide occurs at a serum level of about 100μmol/l. Cyanide is a cellular poison.

Normally the nose acts as a humidifer, warming, filtering and humidifying inspired air. In a patient with a respiratory burn, the nasal mucosa may be damaged and unable to perform this function. Adult respiratory distress syndrome (ARDS) is a condition of respiratory failure with low oxygen pressure despite oxygen administration, increased respiratory rate and tachycardia, which may occur in patients with or without a respiratory burn.

Friction burns occur in road accidents, usually those at low speeds and are due to the exposed soft parts being dragged along the rough surface of the road.

They are rarely deep but are ingrained with dirt and grit. It is essential to remove this by gentle scrubbing before healing occurs in order to prevent permanent tattooing of the skin. In industry, contact with moving belts or wheels may cause skin loss, the seriousness depending on the period of close contact.

3.0 CHAPTER THREE

BURNS FROM CONFLICTS

In large numbers, burn casualties make the combat unit ineffective. Deployment of sophisticated mechanized weaponry such as armoured fighting vehicles (AFVs), armour penetrating explosives and computer guided missiles increase the casualty profile. Penetrating missiles cause the majority of wounds in combat trauma with twice as many penetrations as non-battle injuries (not caused by an enemy). Increasing mechanization in warfare leads to increasing incidence of burn injury. In a fashion similar to that with AFVs, the missile penetration of ships with consequent explosion and fires would create unbearably hot decks and flaming superstructures. Stairs and ladders of aluminum would melt and prevent escape or rescue. Smoke, gases and fumes inhaled from burning of cable insulation and other plastic items as well as from burning paint and rubber materials contribute to higher mortality rates than in less mechanized war arenas. Fuel-air explosive mixtures are common causes of the worst civilian burns disasters. Liquid petroleum gas leakage from storage containers or propylene escape from a ruptured tanker results in tragic explosions injuring thousands.

An aircraft collision on a runway or overshooting the runway can leave hundreds of survivors burned with propellant fuel. Mass casualties resulting from terrorist bombings of innocent civilians usually take place in populous locations, in shopping areas, on buses or trains as exemplified by the activities of terrorists, where vehicle fuel is ignited, burning of victims may be extended beyond the immediate blast locus. Where buildings are bombed or earth quakes destroy buildings there is always the possibility that erupted gas supply lines will create mass burn injuries.

High explosives cause burns especially in a confined space. An urban terrorist bomb of 13.5kg (30 lb) may produce a fireball up to 18 metres (60ft) in diameter. This is immediately dissipated in the open air but the heat is reflected on to the victim in a confined space with solid walls and the air temperature is also raised, superficial flash burns may result. In warfare, injury from incendiary attacks from the air using conventional weapons has produced devastation comparable with attacks with nuclear weapons. Tank crews are particularly at risk from severe burns in modern war. Anti-tank missiles penetrating steel cladding produce fires of intense heat in the enclosed space as well as the release of missile fragments from the inner surface when metal is struck on the outside. The results include severe soft tissue wounds, extensive burns and pulmonary injury.

Napalm is a particularly effective weapon against military targets. Petrol, which is volatile, burns in a relatively, harmless flash. It is modified as a weapon by mixing with additives which change its flow properties. It is thus, cohesive and adhesive, sticking to surfaces as burning gobbets. Rubber was used in the past but aluminum soap obtained from coconut oil, naphthenic acid and oleic acid produces a particularly effective thickner. Napalm (a name derived from aluminum naphthenate and palmitate) is now a generic term for all types of thickened hydrocarbons used as incendiary agents. These include synthetic polystyrene which may be modified further by mixing in other materials such as aluminum powder or metal carbonyls. They produce very high temperatures on burning- well in excess of 1000°C (1832°F) and since they are adhesive, the targets ignite easily. The effect on individuals is devastating. The resultant burns are usually extensive – over 25% of the body surface. The phosphorus present causes toxic injury and the adhesive properties render the material impossible to remove.

Phosphorus burns as encountered on the battlefield or in industry may cause death even if only 12-15% of the body surface is involved. Burning phosphorus causes a lesion which progresses until either all the phosphorus is consumed or the area of the lesion is deprived of oxygen. Pain is severe. The entry of inorganic phosphorus into the bloodstream may give rise to toxic changes. Mustard gas (sulphur mustard) gives off a dangerous vesicant vapour which, with liquid contact, causes blistering of the skin, eye damage and if inhaled, injury to the respiratory tract in individuals. Absorption may cause depression of the bone marrow some 2 weeks after exposure. The healed, blistered skin is characteristically pigmented.

Whereas non- nuclear mass casualties may be quickly evacuated to nearby hospitals for treatment such facilities are unlikely to be available in a nuclear attack. Since intravenous resuscitation for the thermally injured patient will be unavailable, victims with burns in excess of 25 – 30% surface area are unlikely to survive in appreciable numbers. All mass casualties whether from warfare, terrorism or accidents require triage. Triage is the sorting of casualties according to priorities for care to optimize use of medical resources. Triage identifies those with a poor chance of survival, those with a reasonable chance if treated and those with a good chance with no or postponed treatment. Only experience can assess in a short time the chances of life or death of an individual victim. This categorization process is necessary when the casualty needs are excessively out of proportion with the medical means to respond.

Generally, burns occur from miscellaneous sources. Country medicine, prescribed by local medicine man or woman in the form of various potions, salves and heat application, is not only the first line of treatment but may be the source of the burn.

Children, the elderly and the disabled are burn candidates. In the elderly (65-85 + years), flame burns and scalds are most common due to cooking and bathing activities. Many of the injuries result from the general decline in balance, co-ordination and dexterity that accompany old age and falls onto fires and against hot surfaces. Clothing brushing against naked flames and accidents with containers of hot liquids are common causes of thermal injury. In a significant proportion of cases, an event such as a stroke, heart attack or sudden loss of consciousness is the precipitating cause of the thermal injury.

Neurological and physical impairment are predisposing factors to burn injuries. Physicians and other health-care workers often overlook thermal trauma as a hazard to their neurologically and physically disabled patients. A classic example of this oversight is seen with epilepsy. Sensory incoordination and weakness, disorders of mentation and involuntary movements increase the risk of inadvertent mishaps leading to burns. Furthermore, the abilities to recognize and physically withdraw from a potential burn stimulus are impaired by sensory and motor deficits, thereby increasing the duration of such exposure.

There is a higher incidence of burn injuries in paraplegics when compared to the quadraplegic population suggesting that sensory deprivation is a more important risk factor for burn injury. The greater tendency for burns to occur in paraplegics is likely explained by the quadriplegics inability to bathe independently or handle potentially hazardous instruments.

4.0   CHAPTER FOUR

BURNS IN UNDER-AGE

Most burns occur indoors, kitchen and bathrooms being the areas with greatest potential for injury. Seventy percent of childhood burning incidents occur under the age of 5 years with a peak incidence between 1-2 years when children are becoming mobile but have not achieved danger awareness.

Thermal (flame) burns occur in a wide variety of circumstances. Highly mobile toddlers are most at risk. They are curious about everything within reach and attracted by bright objects such as the glass window of an electric oven, the grill of an electric fire or a hot iron but are quite unaware of the dangers of fire or heat. In older children, flammable liquids can cause extensive injury as will clothing catching light from unguarded fire. Flame burns most often result from playing with matches, ignition of flammable liquids and from the lighting of garden fires. Severe burns usually involve the trunk, neck, lower face and result from the ignition of flammable nightwear.

Over the last 20 years, glass fronted gas fires have become a popular addition to many homes. They provide an attractive, clean and efficient means of heat energy. Whilst providing an effective source of heat energy, the flames provide a source of curiosity for children attracting them towards the hot glass plate resulting in contact burns. A contact burn is a burn sustained when a heated object has contact with the skin and produces a defined and localized area of damage. Examples include electric irons, central heating radiators and oven doors as contact hazards. Vacuum cleaners have also been found to be a cause for friction contact burns to the hairs of children. Glass plates can reach up to 245°C in less than quarter of an hour and temperatures can stay up to 50°C for half an hour after switching off the appliance. Accidents with cooking appliances accounted for the majority of contact burns in a domestic setting.

Glass fronted fireplace poses a significant risk, particularly to toddlers. The flames of fires provide an attractive glow to toddlers who can inadvertently touch the glass plates. Burn severity sustained has been shown to be proportional to the temperature of the source, the exposure time and the anatomical distribution of the burn (hands or fingers are the commonest sites involved). Normal reaction time to a painful stimulus is 0.25% second in a healthy adult but this is obviously delayed in those with restricted mobility like toddlers. Most common age group to sustain this type of contact burns in children is between 6months and 3 years. This is most likely due to the developmental stage of the child that is learning to explore, crawl and walk. The palm and fingers are the most risk areas and the depth of burn injury is more of superficial dermal than deep dermal. Petrol is by far the most common flammable agent causing burns accounting for 83% of the cases with aerosols and methylated spirits accounting for 10% and 7% respectively. Petrol and kerosene are the fuels most easily available and most widely used in the world today. Most households have these substances in the gardenshed or basement for domestic use. These fuels have been shown to be the most common flammable liquids that cause burns. The storage of petrol and kerosene in the home is common but there is no government legislation regarding this issue. There is currently no age restriction on the purchase of flammable liquid and no law enforcing the safe storage of these substances.

Children have the innate nature to explore their surrounding environment and to play with new exciting games. Through playing, they acquire skills for survival and develop inter-personal relationships. However, playing with dangerous objects may cause severe injuries to children with serious physical and psychological consequences. Playing with fire is an extremely dangerous behaviours. The burns predominantly affect the head and neck, upper limb, hand and lower limb. Burns also result from firecrackers, wax liquid, domestic iron, domestic cooker, electric bar fire, gas fire, radiator, hot kettle, boiler and light bulb. Domestic iron is the single commonest cause accounting for 46% of cases. Contact burns form a small but important subgroup of the majority of thermal burns occurring in young children. This is due to the fact that contact thermal burns in children frequently affect functionally important sites such as the hand or cosmetically important areas, notably the face.

Palmer burns occur mainly as a result of a child touching a hot object while dorsal burns tend to occur when a hot object falls onto the hand. The contact time tends therefore to be longer for dorsal hand burns and the skin is also thinner. In the hot-iron burns, leaving the iron either on a low table or on the floor has been found to be an important factor in the aetiology of these burns. This particular injury occurs in the young mobile infant predominantly between the ages of 1 and

2 years. The age range in this group is considerable greater although the majority of patients are children under the age of 5 years. Preventive measures to reduce the incidence of contact thermal burns to the hand include encouraging greater parental vigilance and also educating parents to leave a hot iron in a secure place. This could be reinforced by marketing irons with a warning label to keep out of the reach of children. Development of a thermoprotective box in which a hot iron could be placed or the development of irons either with a lower thermal capacity so that they cool quicker or an iron that switches off automatically if not used for some seconds could all be useful steps forward towards reducing the incidence of this potentially serious injury.

Thermal burns to the eye are usually caused by sparks, hot fragments of flying metal or lighted cigarrate. The injury is usually restricted to the epithelium.

Baby walker may aid paediatric injury ranging from minor lacerations and fingertip entrapment to major head injury and death. The scalds were due to the improved reach of the infants with some reaching kettle cords and fresh cup of tea. Burns may account for as little as 2% of baby walker–related injuries.

Scalds are by far the commonest type of burn injury in young children. Most frequently, they involve the lower face and chest. Very young infants who have not begun to walk sustain burns from hot liquids being spilled onto them usually as a result of carelessness on the part of their carers. Toddlers in the age group 1-3 years are exploring their environment continuously and may injure themselves. Scalds contribute some 80% of the total injury in the very young children. These burns may result from upsetting a hot drink or teapot, by reaching up for the projecting handle of a saucepan or by pulling on the cord of an electric kettle, a tablecloth or hot cooking oil. Burns to the buttocks and back can result from hot bath water if the child is left unsupervised even for a very short time and gain access to the hot tap.

Scald burns from hot tap water are paediatric disasters. Although simple precautions could virtually eliminate this major cause of burn morbidity, there is little evidence that the incidence of tap water scald burns has decreased significantly. Several population based studies have suggested that the young are at particular risk of tap water scald burns. Infants are at the greatest risk for scald burns not limited to hot tap water. Tap water scald burns are life threatening injuries.

Accidental Injury to infants can result from the use of home microwave ovens. The spectrum of injury includes scald burns of the trachea, palate and oropharynx due to aspiration and ingestion of foods that have been overheated. There has been a case of a child with second degree burns due to explosion of the plastic liner and nipple on a feeding bottle top. Non accidental burn is possible following placement of infants within microwave ovens.

Several potential accidents may occur if microwave ovens are used to heat milk for infants. The factors involved in scalds secondary to an exploding container are not usually met if the water is heated to 37°C. However it is very easy to accidentally overheat milk. The water in milk is heated more rapidly than the fat particles or protein and is then converted to steam. If this cannot escape because it is within a closed container, the pressure will vent through the teat of the bottle. The power setting of the microwave, the bottle material, the presence or absence of the bottle top during heating, the heating time, the volume of formula and the initial temperature of the formula are all factors that may be altered accidentally, causing unexpected hot milk. Once milk has been overheated in a microwave, it may not be perceived by the child or carer to be as hot as it is, because of the large temperature differential between the surface of the bottle or container and the inner liquid. This is a particular hazard of microwave ovens due to the heating characteristics of this method of preparing milk or food. Despite the recommended policy of not using microwave ovens to heat infant feeds it is still common practice in many homes. Infant formula, prepared baby foods and infant feeding bottles should all have health warnings clearly visible to advise parents of the dangers. In addition, health professionals dealing with children need to be aware of the potential hazards so that appropriate education of parents can take place.

Electrical injuries and burns are common in children. These are usually inquisitive toddlers who poke objects into electric sockets (low voltage burns) or boys of 10-14 years that have wandered onto electrified railway lines (660V D.C) or climbed overhead pylons (high voltage burns). Children come into contact with the domestic electric supply (220 – 250V) and it is the hands which are most frequently affected.

Several factors determine the effects of electrical injury; current (amperage), voltage, whether alternating or direct current, duration of contact, tissue resistance, the path taken, adequacy of earthing and individual characteristics such as sweating. At a current of 5 milliampere (mA), pain is caused and the child will let go of the source of electricity. At 15mA there is titanic muscular construction.. At 30-50 mA, there is powerful contraction of the respiratory muscles and respiratory arrest. Principal sources are overhead power lines, electrified railway lines and lightening.

Current passing through the body takes the line of least resistance from the point of entry to the ground. Wet skin allows more current to enter the body. Electricity flows more readily along nerves, blood vessels and muscle which have the lowest resistance rather than hard tissues, tendon and fat. Most damage tends therefore to occur to nerves and vessels, muscles and skin. Types of electrical burns in children include low voltage contact (<1000 V), high voltage contact (>1000 V) and flash. Electrothermal burns are caused by a young child grasping the hot element of an electric fire. The burn is due to a combination of contact with the hot element and the passage of electric current. There may also be a separate exit burn either on the back of the hand or forearm from earthing on another part of the apparatus. The burns sustained tend to be either partial or full thickness or even deeper burns. Low voltage contacts are usually from the domestic electricity supply or faulty appliances such as plugs, socket or wires. The burns are usually small in size but tend to penetrate deeply and there is often destruction of nerves, bone and joint tissues. Burns at the angle of the mouth are a specific type of low voltage injury. High voltage contact often entails very high voltage (>25000KV). Injury is virtually confined to adolescent boys who climb onto electric pylons, walk on railway lines or throw a wire across electric cables from bridges. Often the injury is in the non-dominant arm which is holding the wire thrown by the dominant arm. Earthing occurs via the feet often unequally depending on the type of footwear. Electric flash burns are usual in children.

Kite-flying is a unique but dangerous mode of electrical injury in children. Kite flying is a popular sport in children and young adults. The kite-flying is associated with various modes of injuries in children like falling from roof and sustaining electrical injuries with high tension current. The resulting burn injuries once sustained produce overwhelming physiological and psychological problems in paediatric victims. The percentage body surface area of burns in cases with current passing through the kite string were significantly less than those seen in other cases probably because string is a poor conductor of electricity transmitting significant current only after it becomes wet. Once the current begins to flow through the tissues, the body acts as a volume conductor. The arcing current ionizes air particles, often raising temperatures to 2500 to 3000°C causing coagulative damage of not only skin but also underlying tendons and other structures. Electrical injuries which are associated with significant morbidity and mortality have a much more severe impact on children who can develop permanent deformities. Long term central nervous system, ophthalmic and skeletal complications can also make life miserable.

Chemical burns in children are the result of accidents in the household. Industrial accidents that occur in adults are much less likely in children. In addition, there may be ingestion. Strong alkali tends to be more damaging than strong acids. Caustic soda, ammonia and concentrated bleach solutions are more notorious. If ingested they cause a chemical gastrointestinal tract. Chemical burns to the eye are a true ophthalmic emergency.

More than half of all accidental deaths are the result of smoke inhalation and many of these occur within the first hour. People trapped in a house fire make frantic efforts to escape and may jump or throw children from upper floor windows. There may also be the effects of blast or crush injuries from falling objects. This can result in further life threatening injuries to the skull, chest, spine and pelvis. Toxic gases perhaps from burning furniture and carbon monoxide may also be inhaled.

Severe sunburn (solar radiation) is common in babies left exposed to sunlight usually early in the summer. A small group of children sustain burns as a form of deliberately inflicted injury. Circular burns of the buttocks or scalds of hands and feet, with well-defined margins, cigarette burns, repeated burn accidents and burns associated with bruises and fractures all arouse suspicion. Some 10% of non-accidental injuries to children may involve some form of localized burn or scald. Epileptics are one particular section of the population at risk. Burns arise during a fit from falling into a fire or as a result of a conflagration caused by overturning a light or heater. There is no attempt to escape from the flames as the victim is unconscious. The burn may therefore, be particularly deep and involve the head or hands.

Splash burns can also be inflicted when scalding liquid is deliberately thrown over a child. Unusual burns include friction. Although they are not a life threatening injury, they are at least as vicious in causing permanent functional and aesthetic disabilities. The combination of two forms of energy released in friction burns, namely mechanical abrasive and scourging thermal, may be the reason behind the marked tissue damaging effect in this type of burn. Most friction burns seem to relate to industrial machinery or traffic accidents but rare with household appliances or in domestic circumstances. The increasing awareness of the value of keep-fit exercises and the upsurge in commercial capitalization on this craze has resulted in numerous appliances flooding the market. The advertising posters showing a happy smiling family using the appliances have created a false sense of safety. The poor design of some jogging machines with no protecting shield to cover the conveyor belt edges and the gap between the belt and the supporting frame is a great hazard to children. The fact that these unfortunate accidents occurred with different brands of machines made in different countries reflects a major problem. It is the responsibility of both the manufacturer and the importing countries to adhere to stricter safety designs in all ranges of this type of machine. User's manuals should also emphasize the risk of injury to children.

Burns of special areas also occur in children. Facial burns are important especially those to the mouth and pharynx because of the risk of airway obstruction. Burns to a hand or foot can cause considerable functional loss and those to the perineum have a tendency to become infected. Circumferential burns affect structures like the chest, the limb or the finger.

Child abuse often results in non-accidental burns. These include circular cigarette stub injuries which tend to be on exposed areas of the body such as the face, arms or legs. Patterned injuries tend to be on parts of the body not used by the child for exploring such as the buttocks. Source of heat may be a hot electric iron or hob or poker. Immersion burns from scalding bath water and splash burns can also be inflicted.

Child abuse by burning contributes significantly to non-accidental injury. While paediatric burn injuries are not the most severe of all paediatric injuries, they consume greater resources in their treatment in terms of length of stay, outpatient follow-up than most other injuries.

Neglect also plays a role in some childhood burns. Some features are specifically suggestive of non-accidental burn injury being due to abuse or neglect: a history inconsistently reported by parent and child, or one which does not adequately explain the injuries noted: a lack of the appropriate parental affect; unwillingness to take responsibility for the child's post burn care: a child aged less than eight months or greater than two years: the existence of other injuries such as fractures: features suggestive of forced immersion (absence of splash marks, clear tide levels, sign of immersion against the base of a hot liquid container, severe uniform burns), or features suggestive of inflicted contact burns.

Social and emotional factors are important in the causes of burns. Many parents have moments of inattention, or lack of awareness of risks, but parents whose personal problems occupy most of their attention or whose lack of education and parenting skills create a high risk environment for the child are the group whose children are more likely to get burned. There is a close association between burns, social deprivation and family stress. Families at greater risk are those living in poverty on subsistence income or being cared for by an unsupported single parent who tends to be young and inexperienced. In such circumstances young children may be entrusted to the care of an older sibling. Children, more often boys may be hyperactive or emotionally disturbed. The house often tends to be of poor quality, over crowded, disorganized and untidy with easy access to dangerous sources of heat or appliances (kettle, oven and hot iron) which are in poor condition. Safety devices are often lacking.

5.0 CHAPTER FIVE

BURNS ASSESSMENT

The assessment of burns accompanied by inhalation injury or associated damage, is a difficult task. The airway, breathing and circulation must be evaluated before the burn wounds in the burned victims.

For every victim who is injured by thermal, chemical, electrical or other trauma, evaluation of the airway has first priority. Victims who have complete airway obstruction will not survive.

The second assessment priority is breathing. The chest of the victim is quickly observed and the quality of breath sounds carefully assessed. The circulation of the patient is also assessed. The presence and adequacy of pulses, radial, femoral or carotid is checked and blood pressure reading obtained. Hypotension in a burn patient is almost invariably caused by hypovolaemia either due to fluid loss into the burned tissues.

5.1 Surface Area Assessment

It is of paramount importance to be able to assess the size of the burn since on this depends the treatment and the prognosis. As the burn size increases, be it partial or full structure involvement especially at the extremities of age, so the mortality increases. All clothing is removed from the patient and the skin completely examined in a warm room. The dimensions of small burns are easily measured but many burns are very large or involve multiple sites. Burn size is usually expressed as the percentage of the total surface area (TBSA) affected. Charts like the Lund and Browder chart are used to assess burns and calculate percentage body surface area affected. The rule of nines is a simple and accurate method of calculating the percentage of the body surface which has been affected; front and back of trunk is assessed 18% each, each leg 18%, each arm 9%, head and neck 9% and genitalia 1%.

Proper estimation of burn size in children is usually more difficult than in adults yet the margin for error in a child is small. Accurate burn size determination is important because of its direct effect on resuscitation, surgical management and prognosis. The 'Rule of Nines' does not apply to children below 15years because of their relatively larger head size and smaller lower limb size. The 'Rule of Tens' is applies: front and back of trunk 20% each, each limb 10% and head and neck 20%. The size of the patient's hand and fingers is 1% of surface area. The Lund and Browder chart divides the various body parts into smaller units such as upper arm, lower arm, hand, leg and others with the necessary adjustments for age.

Burn size estimation is most accurately performed by two people working as a team. One reads the relative percentages for each body part from the chart and records the result while the other person estimates the proportion of that body part burned. It is imperative that burn size and depth estimations be formally reviewed and updated on the second post burn day and again at a later date if necessary.

5.2 Structural Assessment

This is not easy. The thin blistering of the superficial scald and the scorched, coagulated surface of the deep flame burn may be readily distinguished. An added difficulty is due to a large proportion of injuries being of mixed nature with areas of superficial and deep burning shading into each other. The history provides a guide, simple thermal trauma e.g. sunburn, hot liquids, flash burns from petrol or gas explosions cause a superficial burn while boiling water, molten metals, house fires, burning clothes, falling on fires and cooker while unconscious cause structural damage.

The temperature of the burning agent and the time of the exposure determine both the depth of burning and the appearance of the skin surfaces seen soon after the injury. Nevertheless the appearance of the burn usually allows at least a tentative assessment to be made. At this stage, some burns will be obviously superficial, some obviously deep and some of doubtful depth and in some burns, areas of the three types will be present (mixed).

Simple blistering is suggestive of superficial damage. At times the superficial layers of the skin are lost and the deeper layers are pink and viable indicating partial structural loss. The burn which is dark brown or black with a translucent appearance and clouded vessels involves the entire structures of the skin. Generally, the thicker the skin showing this appearance the more likely that some viable epithelial elements remain. Some burns like burns by hot liquids are difficult to classify initially but with time a true assessment is made..

Since the sensory end organs are concentrated in the skin, the presence of sensation indicates that part of the skin is viable, while absence of sensation suggests whole skin destruction. Touch is unsuitable as a form of sensation for testing, but the presence of pain on pricking with a pin (pinprick test) is valuable evidence of the existence of a viable layer of the skin. The test is performed by pricking the skin firmly with a sterile pin or needle. The test is positive if the patient complains of feeling pain. For the test to be negative, it must be possible to drive the pin right through the skin into the subcutaneous fat without causing pain.

A positive reaction to pinprick is definite evidence of the presence of viable cells but a negative reaction cannot be interpreted so firmly because, particularly in areas with a naturally low sensitivity, the pin can be driven right through the skin into the subcutaneous fat without causing pain, yet viable skin cells are still present and the skin will heal. The skin of the face is an example of this.

Other special methods to assess the depth of burning are temperature measurements, thermography, intravital dye injections and isotope uptake

In children, burn depth is usually very difficult to estimate especially in the early post burn period. This is, in large part, due to the thinness of a child's skin. The depth of scald burns especially in dark skinned infants is difficult to estimate. Underestimation of burn depth often occurs even with experienced observers. Burn depth must be re-evaluated several times weekly to determine both prognosis and the need for surgical intervention.

Burn depth can also be assessed by measurement of the skin blood flow using a Laser Doppler Scanner. The scanner is controlled by an IBM-type computer which also acts as an image storing and display a scale of blood flow.

The principle of laser doppler flowmetry is to measure the doppler shift, that is the frequency shift that light waves undergo when reflected by moving objects such as red blood cells. A proportion of the laser beam is back scattered from stationary structures which remain at its original frequency and therefore the reflected laser light picked up by the photodiodes is a combination of doppler shifted and non-shifted light which is processed into an arbitrary scale of blood flow.

Laser doppler perfusion imaging (LDPI) is a further development in laser doppler flowmetry (LDF). Its advantages are that it enables assessment of microvascular blood flow in a predefined skin area rather than, as for LDF, in one place. In many ways this method seems to be more promising than LDF in the assessment of burn wounds. The blood flow in injured tissue indicates the extent of tissue damage. Superficial second degree burns have perfusion values greater than those of normal skin whereas the perfusion in deep second degree and third degree burns is compromised. Microvascular blood flow and the depth of burn is assessed by LDPI.

Perfusion of burn wounds assessed by LDI is related to burn depth and healing time. Superficial burns have a better preserved and more active microcirculation compared to deeper burn wounds. A method for assessing skin perfusion helps to make correct burn depth estimation. A new method for evaluating the depth of burns by imaging the blood flow through the burned tissue using fluorescence from intravenously injected indocyanine green (ICG) dye.

Burn depth can also be established by measurement of surface temperature. Diagnosis of burn depth is usually based on a combination of the history of the injury and the surface appearance of the wound with addition of the pinprick test. The early surface appearance of the burn is largely determined by the state of the superficial dermal capillaries and the blood in them. Direct measurement of surface temperatures was by using rapidly responding skin thermocouple probes connected to an electrical meter reading to 0.1°C.

Surface temperature does not appear to be a reliable guide to the depth of burn if the measurements are made a few hours after injury. This may be because of progressive changes occurring in the dermal capillaries. Alterations in the peripheral circulation are responsible for differing relationships between the surface temperature of burned and unburned skin.

This method of diagnosis has several advantages. It is easy for the doctor and painless for the patient. It takes only a few minutes to make the necessary readings The disadvantages include being unsuitable for large areas of burn as there is no normal skin nearby for comparison. It is also inappropriate for certain areas of the body. In some cases, these problems may be overcome by comparing the burn with the corresponding area on the opposite side of the body. The method also seems to be unreliable for burns seen late. As with any means of assessment, some readings are borderline and the method should be used in conjunction with other forms of clinical assessment. The method is useful in patients mainly children who are not suitable for the pinprick test.

Infrared thermography is another method for investigating burns which affect skin blood flow. The damage to skin blood vessels caused by thermal injury is a major determinant of the capacity of the wound to heal. Thermographic assessment of this damage has been found to correlate with the healing time of burn wounds.

Thermography has the potential for the investigation of burn depth. However, the surface of the wound cools due to evaporative water loss

The measurement of burn depth is not exact.. There is some agreement in the criteria used for the clinical assessment of burn depth. However, the complexity of the dynamic changes that occur to the cellular elements of skin post-burn has resulted in the failure to produce an agreed technique for the histological measurement of burn depth.

Evaluation of burn depth is important in planning the management of the burn wound. Burn depth is most commonly evaluated clinically by assessment of appearance, blanching, capillary return and evaluation of sensation. The use of histologic sections is the gold standard with which the accuracies of other technique are compared.

6.0   CHAPTER SIX

BURNS CATEGORIES

Burns are classified according to depth of structures affected. These are surface burns, partial structural burns and entire structural burns.

Surface burn

These burns do not affect true structures of the skin except the surface outer layers. The hair follicles, sebaceous glands and the sweat glands are not affected Recovery is good and fast and in due time presents an appearance similar to normal.

Partial structural burn

The first and second layers of skin are affected notably the dermis and the sebaceous glands while the sweat glands are spared. Recovery is not fast and uneventful as tissue damage extends to the subcutaneous tissue. Scars appear on the healed skin.

Entire structures burn

The entire skin is lost. Structures deeper than skin, fat fascia, sweat gland, muscle or even bone are damaged. Hospitalization is prolonged; treatment is intensive and outcome unpredictable. Physiological mechanisms are severely affected and disrupted. Possible healing and recovery is not without scar formation.

The extent of injury depends on the amount of surface area burnt, the depth and location of injury, the age and general condition of the patient and the presence or absence of concomitant injury. Victims with renal or heart disease are poor subjects as well as those at either extreme of life, that is the very young or the very old. Surface area involvement is calculated by the rule of nine. This is rapid, though not very accurate. In infants, the head area is much larger than the rule of nine allows while the lower limb area is much smaller. The reverse is true for adults. In children, the rule of five or ten is used in calculating the surface area involved in burns.

Since severity of injury is related to the amount of tissue lost, surface burns are not as severe as other types of burn.

On basis of severity, surface burns covering 20% of the body surface area and above, 10% TBSA in a victim over age 50, 10%TBSA in underage are regarded as major burns while less than 10%TBSA in victims between ten and fifty years constitute minor burns that do not require hospitalization.

Some burns are judged as severe in spite of small surface area involvement. These are burns of the face, hands, feet and external genitalia. This is seen in burns that occur in closed environments such as cinemas, houses and on board ship or in burns of the face that occur during periods of unconsciousness as in epileptics.

Prognosis in burns is not easy. Advanced age, extensive surface area involvement, increased depth of the lesion and/or previous ill-health imparts negatively on progress.

7.0 CHAPTER SEVEN

BURNS BIOCHEMICAL MECHANISM

Burns initiate pathological changes and an untreated victim goes into a state of shock. Any depth of skin may be destroyed but deeper layers, although still viable, will be severely affected by the heat. The capillaries are dilated and as the permeability of the walls increases, protein-rich fluid is rapidly lost from the plasma into the extracellular space causing a loss of circulating blood volume. At the same time there is blister formation and further fluid loss if the surface of the burn is moist. The rate of loss of fluid is rapid for some hours but slows over the following 2 to 3 days when reabsorption of fluid occurs. In addition to capillary wall damage, there is damage to the red blood cells trapped at the moment of burning; this corresponds to the blood loss in other injuries. Fortunately, plasma loss, initially rapid, slows over the first 48 hours and is only slight after this. In this first critical period there is massive fluid loss in the form of plasma and some blood loss due to direct thermal trauma to red blood cells. Complement activation may lead to release of oxygen radicals.

The liver cell is especially liable to injury because of its function of taking up and dealing with many toxic substances or chemicals.

The symptoms of the shock phase are related to the extent of the area of skin burned and not to the depth of burning. The loss of protein- rich fluid from the plasma at the site of the burn is the factor of over- riding importance in the causation of the clinical condition of shock in burn patients. The fluid loss results in a fall in plasma volume and because there is proportionately less loss of protein than electrolyte solution, there occurs a slight rise in osmotic pressure.

Hypovolaemic (oligaemic) shock is due to loss of blood volume. In burns, oligaemic shock is due to loss of plasma into the skin and subcutaneously in the burned area. Septic shock (bacteraemia) is caused by endotoxins of Gram-negative bacteria. These endotoxins cause loss of tone in small blood vessels which consequently dilate. The blood vessels dilate and normal blood volume is not adequate for effective circulation. The shock of fright and pain is of this type. A free radical is a molecule with an unpaired electron in the outer orbit and is capable of an independent transient existence. This odd electron is frequently represented by a dot ($\cdot$) in chemical formulas (e.g. O_2^- $OH\cdot$) and imparts a potent oxidizing and/or reducing potential to the molecular species (i.e., it receives or donates electrons respectively). The major pathway of oxygen metabolism that occurs in man involves the tetravalent reduction of molecular oxygen by the cytochrome oxidase system in the mitochondria with the resultant production of ATP and water. Only 1 to 2% of oxygen substrate may leak from the system to become metabolized by univalent reduction producing various oxygen radicals. Free radicals are formed by the hemolytic cleavage of a covalent bond of a normal molecule with each fragment retaining one of the paired electrons, by the loss of a single electron to a normal molecule and by the addition of a single electron to a normal molecule. Free radicals can be positively charged, negatively charged or electrically neutral.

The most important free radicals in biological system are radical derivative of oxygen. The addition of one electron to the oxygen molecule results in the superoxide radical. The addition of two electrons yields hydrogen peroxide. Hydrogen peroxide is not a free radical but is also referred to as a reactive oxygen specie that includes not only oxygen free radicals but also non-radical oxygen derivatives that are involved in oxygen radical production. Hydrogen peroxide is an important compound in free radical biochemistry because it is easily broken down, particularly in the presence of transition metal ions to produce the most reactive and damaging of the oxygen free radicals, the hydroxyl radical.

. During normal body conditions there exists a balance between free radicals and the natural scavengers of the body, but during traumatic state the balance is lost and reactive oxygen metabolites outnumber. At this stage therapeutic application of enzymatic and non-enzymatic antioxidants becomes impreative.

Attempts to reach an understanding of the basic causes of death from burns have focused on the one consistent element, the percent TBSA for a given age. The burned surface area is related inversely to survival chance but the younger the brighter the survival.

8.0   CHAPTER EIGHT

BURNS VICTIMS CONVEYANCE

The conveyance of the burn victim is divided into primary transport, from the site of injury to the receiving hospital and secondary transport, from the receiving hospital to the specialist burn unit. From the site of the accident transport should obviously be by the swiftest means practicable to the nearest hospital casualty department. Care must be taken to avoid any additional injury.

An ambulance or car transport may be available for transfer to an accident department a few miles but air transport should be considered when long distances are involved for those without con-indication. Before the transfer, the severity of injury is immediately assessed in cases of mass burn. The number of casualties must be ascertained and a formal triage performed. It is vitally important to maintain body temperature but contaminated clothing must be removed. If clothing has been removed, foil blankets or other warm coverings must be used to conserve body heat. Stabilization of the victim before transport is necessary for life threatening cases. However, victims with internal injuries will benefit from rapid, skillful transfer to the receiving hospital where specialist treatment can be instituted. The patients must be monitored throughout the journey. Transfer itself can worsen the existing deleterious physiological changes therefore it is important to communicate with the driver so that the speed of the vehicle can be adjusted to the needs of the patient. It is still commonly held belief that the faster the driver, the better the outcome, this is not necessarily the case.

Secondary conveyance occurs between the receiving hospital and a specialist centre, in this case a Burn unit. Before secondary transfer, it is important that the patient is fully assessed and resuscitated Biochemical and haematological parameters are documented because of the risk of ignoring unsafe data as very abnormal result like serum potassium may lead to fatal outcome.

Airway problems need managing definitively prior to transport. It is unacceptable to allow the development of airway obstruction during transfer. The risks of transfer must be balanced very carefully against the possible benefit. There is no room for impulsive actions. It is the responsibility of the personnel transporting the patient to ensure that all necessary equipment is present and in full working order. The equipment taken must be sufficient to allow the management of most eventualities. Enough oxygen must be present, not only for the transfer but making allowance for unforeseen delays. A formal written summary of the injuries and management is presented to the receiving team upon arrival. All relevant documentation including investigation results and x-rays must be carefully packaged and accompany the victim.

9.0 CHAPTER NINE

BURNS MICROBIAL INFECTION

Burns are open wounds and are easily liable to invasion by bacteria. It is a major factor contributing to death and remains so in spite of the development of new and more effective antibiotics. There is more to an infection than identification of the causative agent. There are three components to an infection: the host, the infecting organism and the timing. Each component has the elements of being qualitative, quantitative and dynamic. The skin has four major functions: to keep heat inside the body, to keep water inside the body, to keep invading organisms outside the body and to give contour to the body. Care for a burn victim is to these functions. Of the four, keeping invading oganisms under control is the most difficult. The immunological consequences of a burn are far reaching. Once the injury is larger than 10 to 15% total body surface area in size, the physiological impact is no longer local but affects distant and systemic protective mechanisms. Burn patients can have early infection from unusual circumstances but usually become infected at 5 to 7 days post - injury.

Infecting agents originate from two locations, from inside or outside the body. Those from inside the body can come from several areas. As a consequence of the burn injury, bacteria can spread systemically if not controlled by intrinsic or extrinsic mechanisms. Intrinsic bacteria can come from localized abscess, an infected lung, a urinary tract infection or the gut. The deranged immunological function that occurs as a consequence of the burn can release an otherwise controlled infection allowing it to progress and spread. The concern now is burn victims with human immunodeficiency virus (HIV) Infection. Their condition does not improve and burning can initiate a cascade of complications.

Infections originating from the outside (extrinsic organisms) come from two locations: The general environment and from the caregivers. Infection from the environment may begin at the same time as the burn occurs. The caregivers may contaminate a patient during the giving of care by spreading organisms originating from themselves or from one patient to another. As bacteria are passed from one animal to another there is a selection of the virulent form of an organism. In a burnward, there are times when a specie of bacteria becomes common to several patients. This occurs because a resident organism contaminates several patients.

People and the equipment they use to care for burn patients can be a source of infection. During transport to a hospital, a patient with a large burn will frequently have intravenous lines placed by transport personnel. These are done with the haste of an emergency and as life-saving manoeuvres. They are not always done with the best of sterile techniques. Similar manoeuvres occur in the emergency room. Clothes that brush against an infected wound can carry organisms to a distant site. Hands unwashed are both historical and current causes for passing infections among patients. Food given to patients to improve and aid recovery can be dangerous. Fresh vegetables and fruits are contaminated with organisms and must be cooked before being given to susceptible patients. Standing water becomes easily contaminated. The water in which flowers are kept, even plant soil harbours bacteria. None of these must be allowed in the burn centre. This policy also applies to non-patient areas, for a staff member can become contaminated and pass organisms around the unit. Contaminated equipment passed from one patient to another can convey bacteria, selecting a virulent form of the organisms that begins to kill patients. Techniques must be in place at all times in the burn centre to prevent cross contamination.

Intrinsic organisms arise from so many sources. Flora from the gastrointestinal (GI) tract, the respiratory tree, the vagina and the skin contaminate wounds. Burn wound dressings are changed in a variety of ways. Some are done in rooms designed exclusively for wound care. Others are changed at the time of bathing. Not all dressing are done outside the patient's rooms, many are changed while the patient is in bed because the condition of the patient is critical. This is not the best condition, for the bedding and the content of the room are always contaminated. A patient having bowel movements in bed is soiling his wounds continually. A patient coughing up infected sputum continually inoculates his wounds.

The skin participates in the general immunological response, it's by -products are used throughout the body. It regulates temperature by giving off heat as well as conserving it, it absorbs substances, excretes substances and it breathes. The skin is the barrier to the outside world and when it is gone the outside world enters unwanted. The goal of the burn team is to re-establish this barrier.

Burn wound sepsis is regarded as 100,000 organisms per gram of tissue. The quantitative measurement of bacteria in the wound has become an integral part in the clinical care and a positive wound culture is definitive of sepsis in burn patients. Stapylococcus epidermidis is a clinical pathogen for burn patients. Staphylococcus aureus is a frequent resident in burn wounds, often resident in burn wards, often resistant to methicillin and thought to be a hospital-acquired infection. Staph aureus is a present problem but is not a new one. There is a cycle whereby organisms appear, disappear and reappear in the burn wards. The phenomenon is a consequence of changing antibiotics and the prolonged survival of patients with large wounds.

A non-bacterial organism which infects debilitated burn victims is the candida species. Its presence is an bad sign for a burn victim and is indicative of severe immunological compromise. Candida may be heralded by staph epidermis infection in the wounds or in blood. Herpes is a viral infection seen in children and adults.

10.0   CHAPTER TEN

BURNS IDENTITY

The major adverse fallouts of healed burns are hypertrophic or keloid scar formation and scar contracture both of which can cause severe disfigurement and functional disability. The initial result of the healing of burns, with or without skin grafting, may be acceptable but over the ensuing months the soft areas of healed epithelium become increasingly livid, indurated and raised above the surrounding normal skin and contract across surfaces. This contracture always limits the range of movement but may be so severe as to dislocate joints.

The extent of scarring depends on the depth and site of the burn as well as the age of the victim. In surface burns, there may be some depigmentation of the area which gradually returns to normal. Partial and entire structural burns result in scar formatiom at the margins of grafts and in areas which have healed by secondary epithelialization. Burn scars are initially flat and fairly inconspicuous, then red, thick and hard and finally flat, white and soft.

Hypertrophic scar occurs with prolonged intensity and duration of the hardness. In entire structural burns hypertrophic scarring is a common outcome, reaching maximum intensity about three months after healing when the scar becomes static for a period and gradually resolves over one to two years, becoming pale, soft and flat. Often the scar is intensively itchy in the active phase and there is a racial or familial predisposition to heavy scarring. The quality of the healed skin is much improved and hypertophic scarring is minimal if the deep dermis is preserved either by preventing extension of the depth of the burn by controlling infection or by achieving early healing. Though hypertrophic scarring is common and expected with extensivel burns, it is usual for the scars gradually to become paler, softer and flatter from five to twelve months but remain as permanent blemishes.

True keloid scars are rare and very difficult to treat. Essentially they are identical in their early stages to hypertrophic scars but unlike the latter they are progressive and tend to involve adjacent undamaged skin. Keloids are secondary to wounds that are deeper than the epidermis. There are body reactions to an altered dermal constituent probably altered by injury.

Social consequences include disfigurement, loss of earnings, social isolation and destruction of marriages as well as dependence, depression and eventual stress disorder.

11.0   CHAPTER ELEVEN BURNS

EMOTIONAL DISPLAY

A burn injury is almost an unexpected event. With significant injury comes significant pain. The response of the patient and staff to the pain and the effects of the medication given for pain relief all have a major impact on the victims emotional display. The impact of the injury on the central nervous system also influences the psychological response of the patient. The presence of a clouded sensorium and of cognitive deficits all affects the psychological experience of the injured patient.

In the acute phase of severe injury there is an initial period of withdrawal. This withdrawal occurs with a large burn, loss of limb or serious threat to life. Although this reaction is common to the majority of injured victims, children in particular, are likely to exhibit this behaviour. The withdrawing victim shows little interest in external events due to a combination of psychological conservation withdrawal reaction and an ego defense mechanism of denial. A conservation withdrawal response is an emotional state characterized by decreased interaction with the environment, decreased energy, decreased activation of bodily systems and immobilization and subsides within one to two weeks after the injury but may persist when there is sustained physiological threat to the victim's life. The preoccupation with pain, dressing changes, traction and laboratory visits take up most of the physical and psychological energy of the patient.

Defense mechanism of denial manifests when the victim denies the extent of the injury, the loss of a body part, the loss of function, the loss of life or injury to others or the loss of home or other significant property. The victim accepts the loss of limb but fails to show the expected concern about this major loss. A victim of functional disability with expectations to go home or return to work in a short time is most likely displaying the defense mechanism of denial.

Denial is an artificial protective defense mechanism but its self deceit and unwillingness to accept reality like the possibility of death, mutilation and pain. Denial leads to wrong decisions, refusal of necessary medication and scheduled surgeries, desire to leave hospital and inability to plan realistically ahead.

Most victims who are admitted show some degree of psychological regression and return to an early way of coping with stress. They are assertive, demanding and with little temper control.

At times anger and hostility manifest since the victim has temporarily lost limbs, body image, possessions, loved ones and control of urination. Head trauma affects the victim's behaviour and anger expressed at the actual target of anger or directed onto another person.

Anxiety emerges because the victim perceives the injury as a hopeless situation that reawakens basic fears. After the burn incident, the sense of seeing oneself as being fully intact is lost. This means that the sense of wholeness is shattered.

The fear for strangers is not ruled out as the victim places his or her fate in the hands of stranger and aliens whose actions arouse insecurity concern. Hospitalization leads to separation from family and friends bringing out separation anxiety. Prolonged hospitalization increases separation and anxiety. Being seriously injured also brings out fears about death and dying meaning separation from loved ones. Victims burned and disfigured are greatly concerned about losing their attractiveness and functional ability especially castration in males and obvious mutilation in females. The victims in hospital have their bodies exposed, probed and weakened, making them susceptible to anxiety that comes injuries which may be increased with injuries to the eyes, face, genitals and breasts.

Some burn victims perceive the burn event as a repercussion of earlier acts of omission or commission and express feelings of guilt, shame and depression. Badly burned victims regard themselves as disfigured entity or a helpless and hopeless cripple.

12.0 CHAPTER TWELVE

BURNS MANAGEMENT

Burns are common injuries managed by members of different specialists including general practitioners, casualty officers, general and orthopaedic surgeons with bias in traumatology, and plastic surgery.

An ambulance or any available vehicle called to the site of the event drives the victims to the nearest health care facility. Ideally burn victims are initially attended to by a general practitioner, the casualty officer or in rare case by the specialist of a nearby clinic or hospital. After resuscitation and stabilization those with partial or entire structural injuries are transferred to a burn centre to be admitted and managed by a team of specialists including dietary experts.

Burns management is an intensive care with a definite protocol carried out with the highest level of professionalism. There is no room for wrong decision, procrastination or negligence and all health professionals are members of the burn care team for adequate and successful treatment. It is important that all necessary facilities are provided in a burn centre including regular power supply, water and blood banking service. Badly burned victims require an isolation ward or intensive care unit while those with less serious injuries can be accommodated in a common burn ward with well spaced beds.

Children are admitted in a separate ward with facilities that are children friendly in a typical burn centre. Close relatives are allowed to attend to children for better care and to drive away fear of insecurity. Prognosis is better in children than in the elderly. Small-size hospitals can accommodate both children and adults together.

The accommodation recognizes the two phases of the burn illness - the shock period and the healing period. Some victims are admitted soon after the injury not yet contaminated with pathogenic organisms, but may be in danger of developing shock. Therefore adequate space and general hygiene are paramount with provision for washing, air-conditioner, oxygen supply and operating theartre. It is desirable to install television sets to ease tension and boredom and if possible recreational parks for adults and children. This enhances battered morale.

Due to inadequate facilities necessary for optimum treatment of each type of injury in some centres initial sorting is recommended but no rejection on the basis of age, extent of injury or expected outcome. Ad hoc burn wards are created when necessary and staff mobilized in times of great challenge as it's unprofessional to transfer or reject some victims to die in order to admit potential survivors. For life -threatening cases, the victims are given first class treatment in special accommodation to ensure the best chance of survival especially for those with inhalation injury.

Injuries of up to 20 percent of the body surface qualify as disabling burns but not life threatening. In mass casualty situation, additional staff with a good knowledge of burns care may be engaged.

Some victims are treated as outpatients depending on the size of the disaster but in civilian disasters the number of outpatients are large and provides an immense load for the hospital which must rise above the challenge.

13.0   CHAPTER THIRTEEN

BURNS DEMANDS

Total recovery from burns is a long process which can be prolonged and aggravated by complications. Overall costs of care of victims of burns is high as it depends on lengthy stays and demands multidisplinary teams of nurses, surgeons psychiatrists, intensive care physicians, psychologists, medical laboratory scientists, nutritionists and physiotherapists.

Improvements in burn care enable us to save many lives of burn victims that were not salvageable in the past. The possibility of saving the lives of extensively burned victims attracted enormous financial implication for the affected.

Costs imply the size and depth of the burned area, the quality of bathing and dressing and complications if any. Cost is definitely high for victims with partial and entire structural injuries because of intensive care including special diets and prolonged hospitalization.

Cost effective regulations should be adopted to shorten hospital stay through aggressive treatment and nutritional support. In advanced burn centers the average hospital stay per victim is one day per percent burn. This is practicable by adopting prompt aggressive policies of surgery, nursing, nutrition, physiotherapy and occupational therapy

14.0   CHAPTER FOURTEEN

BURNS LABORATORY

Prompt laboratory evaluation and subsequent monitoring of burn victims are most essential for their survival because burns initiates a series of pathophysiological changes, the magnitude of which if not reversed may lead to unpleasant outcome. A comprehensive investigation will always guide the team of clinicians in the right path to success especially with the major burns and even minor burns with complications.

Haemoglobin, the red pigment that carries and distributes oxygen in the body must be estimated because of the hypoxia that accompany burns in addition to the packed cell volume measurement that indicates the ratio of blood cells to plasma volume. Haematological changes occur in burns, therefore a full blood count is required to assess and monitor deviations from normal physiology.

Burns are accompanied with significant fluid and protein loss with re-arrangement of electrolytes creating a shift in the internal milieu. The electrolyte balance of the body is distorted and this gives rise to disequilibrium of the acid – base status of the victims. Blood levels of potassium, sodium, chloride and bicarbonate should be monitored regularly to tackle respiratory or metabolic abnormalities that may arise. A complete kidney function profile assesses changes in kidney clearance ability to avoid accumulation of unwanted wastes.

Protein fractions re-arrangement is common in burns with reversed albumin-globulin ratio. Protein electrophoresis is required for total view and assessment of protein abnormality. Myoglobin, uric acid, calcium and adenosine triphosphate levels are additional biochemistry measurements to avoid acute intracellular dysfunction in multiple organs. Some hospitalized patients at times manifest jaundice necessitating periodic liver function evaluation and urine analysis to check for discolouration, presence of protein and intact or haemolysed red blood cells.

Burns victims also require blood and urine cultures as some of them develop septicaemia and infection of internal organs especially by opportunistic organisms due to compromised immune status of these victims.

The significant loss of fluid and subsequent hypoxia leads to a disturbance of normal homeostasis. This makes it imperative to estimate thyroid hormones, whose function in the body is the maintenance of normal homeostatic mechanism. Thus, assessment of thyroid stimulating hormone (TSH), free and bound thyroxine (FT4 and T4), free and bound thyronine (FT3 and T3), and reversed thyronine (rT3) are all important. In our study with over eighty victims, we discovered an imbalance in the levels of these hormones following burns.

15.0   CHAPTER FIFTEEN

BURNS AVOIDANCE

Burns by fire, hot liquids and contact with hot surfaces have been recognized as significant hazards for centuries. Historically many fire disasters resulted not only in property loss but also in considerable loss of life. The mortality from burn injuries is decreasing in economically developed countries due to regulations and improved burn treatment. Burn injuries continue to be a major public health problem in other countries especially economically developing countries.

15.1 Avoidance Measures

There are three man strategies to reduce harm from injuries: education, which primarily is an active measure requiring behaviour/lifestyle change and product design/environmental change and legislation and regulation. The approach for effective burn avoidance in a particular area is based on sound knowledge of the prevalent causes burn injury, geographical variations and socioeconomic differences. Passive protective measures include product modification, environmental redesign or control and legislation while active measures are persistent, long-term behavioural or lifestyle change. Of utmost importance is public education and promotion of legislation. Education is quite important to mitigate the severity of the injury, such as the recommendation to "stop, drop and roll", "apply cool water to a burn injury", and "crawl under smoke".

15.2 Avoidance of Burns from Hot Water

Tap water scalds tend to be more severe than other scalds, involving a larger percentage of the body surface area and frequently leading to skin grafting and hypertrophic scarring.

The avoidance of tap water burns is apparent: lower the temperature setting of the water heater to between 120 and 130° F (49-54°C), a temperature range that is relatively safe but provides an adequate water temperature for household needs. For some countries, educational campaign to lower the temperature setting on water heaters resulted in some many requests to local utility companies for reduction of household water temperature settings. Educational efforts to prevent tap water burns and passive avoidance strategies, not requiring correct behaviour by the potential victim are all effective in injury control.

Recommended measures to avoid hot water scald burns include the use of large round handles or push- and- turn type handles to prevent young children from turning on the hot water and the installation of antiscald showerheads but these measures are not useful for preventing domestic scalds for people whose domestic hot water source is other than a water heater and tap. Commonly the injury pattern involves children falling into open containers of boiling hot water, heated by a fire, or having water from such containers spilled onto them. Effective avoidance control measures for these burns involve building an elevated hearth for the fire, and physically separating children from the heating/cooking area. since cultural habits, lifestyle and bathing systems contribute to hot water-related burns.

15.3 Avoidance of Burns from Fires

House fires are responsible not only for property loss but also for major burn injuries. Most residential fires are caused by smoking materials and lighters, heating equipment and electrical malfunction, cooking and children playing with matches. Young children, the elderly and individuals who are differently disabled are at highest risk for residential fire deaths. Effective public health strategies to reduce residential fire related injuries include installation of a working smoke or fire alarm, use of an automatic sprinkler system, the design and practice of a fire escape plan.

Smoke detector installation is an effective and inexpensive strategy to reduce residential fire deaths by providing early warning. Although smoke detectors provide early warning to reduce injuries by allowing occupants to escape or to defend themselves from fire, young children, the elderly and people who cannot escape unaided continue to be victims of the fire even when they have been alerted by an alarm. Automatic sprinklers are ideal passive protection for these populations. Automatic sprinklers are designed to control or extinguish a developing fire to offer occupants an improved opportunity to escape or not escape as well as to reduce property loss. The fire is extinguished before the concentration of combustion products becomes fatal. No multiple loss of life due to fire or smoke has taken place in fully sprinkled buildings. In addition, property loss is minimal.

Elimination of ignition sources like cigarettes, matches and lighters is also a preventive measure. Cigarettes are the primary ignition source for fatal fires. Common occurrences are a cigarette drops falls into upholstered furniture where it smolders and starts a fire several hours later, and a smoker falls asleep in bed, often after drinking alcoholic beverages, the cigarette falls on the bedding, smolders and ignites the mattress. Other home fires occur when a cigarette ignites paper, curtains or clothing. The obvious control strategy is to modify the cigarette itself, either by lowering the temperature and/or length of time a cigarette burns. The idea of making cigarettes to be self-extinguishing is unacceptable by tobacco companies because of reduced returns.

Children playing with matches or lighters are another cause of house fires. Measures to reduce the chances that matches or lighters start fires include placing the striking surface on the back of match books to prevent unintentional ignition of the entire book, producing matches that are difficult for children to light or fragment, self extinguishing child-resistant lighters.

15.4 Avoidance of Burns from Chemicals

While many chemicals primarily pose toxic risks, more than 25,000 chemicals causing burns injury have been identified. Many of these chemicals are oxidizing agents, reducing agents, or corrosives. In addition, educational programs stress copious cool water irrigation on injured areas immediately after contact with certain chemicals. Hazardous materials are handled professionally with all protective gadgets in place. It is advised that all harmful chemicals and medicines be kept out of the reach of children.

15.5 Avoidance of Burns from Electricity

Burns caused by electricity are relatively small, but these injuries are often deep and require surgery and can be extensive especially if high – voltage or lightning is involved or if clothing ignition occurs. For the common household current such as electrical wiring, the use of a ground fault circuit interrupter (GFCI) is beneficial, shutting off the electrical current to the outlet if a short or current leakage is detected along an unintended path. Avoidance measures include redesign of electrical plugs and the use of covers for electrical outlets while prevention strategies for high-voltage burns include burying power lines, making open wires, live rails and transformer substations less accessible and undertaking educational efforts to reduce risk-taking behaviours. Thunderstorms are dangerous and not safe for people under tall trees in open places. They must stay indoors. Electrical wire connections should not be tampered but repaired by certified personnel.

Avoidance measures include;

1. The positioning of hot liquids on shelves or table tops should be out of reach of the toddler or crawler and the removal of table cloths which may be dragged off the table bringing dangerous liquids with them.

2. The exclusion of children from the kitchen or bathroom, by gates if necessary.

3. The equipping of all kitchens with fire-resistant clothes or towels

4. The installation of guard rails round the tops of gas and electric ovens

5. The fitting of secured fire guards round open fires

6. The avoidance of trailing electric flexes attached to kettles

7. Ceiling mounting of electric light switches cords in bathrooms

8. The locking of domestic bleaches and cleansers away from the reach of children, in safety stoppered bottles.

9. Prohibition of smoking in bed in old people's homes or hospitals.

10. The fitting of domestic electrical sockets with safety cut-outs

16.0 CHAPTER SIXTEEN

RECOMMENDATION

Burns are avoidable accidents in most cases. Many developing countries seem to concentrate more on therapy than on prevention. This is a wrong approach to the problem. Education is the mainstay of burn prevention. This includes making children and parents realize the danger of careless handling of fire and fire-causing materials like matches. In many homes, cooking over an open fire is commonplace, such cooking is done at floor level and there is no guard for the open flames. These situations encourage burn accidents. Cooking should be at a higher level which the children cannot easily reach and the position of the fire should be such that it cannot be easily overturn. Cooking should be done with vessels that can be easily handled, not handless pots.

Avoidance campaigns have been developed to educate the public about behaviours related to burn injury. Some educational programs typically the more focused programs have succeeded in lowering burn injury incidence and severity. The success of educational programs include careful analysis of burns and fire cases in the area, timely modification to cover new information identified by indepth investigations of fire episodes, the intensive and extensive long educational campaign and the focus on one type of burn injury. In addition, behavioural and environmental changes to prevent fire related burns could be adopted without major changes in lifestyle. Publicity or education is given, through television, radio, newspaper, magazines, school initiated program and community outreach program.

In spite of the landmarks in burn avoidance, it remains painfully clear that people living in poor economic situations suffer disproportionately from burn injuries as well as from many other types of injuries and diseases. To prevent burn injuries, programs that alleviate poverty, overcrowding, family stress and educational deficits and that target high risk people living in these conditions are imperatives as well as programs to reduce morbidity and mortality worldwide. Burns remain an important public health issue throughout the world, especially in the economically developing countries. Socioeconomic status plays a strong risk factor for burn injury.

All burn associations such as the Burn Awareness coalition, the American Academy of Paediatrics, National fire protection Association, Burn prevention foundation, Consumer product safety commission, National Safe Kids Campaign and many other interest-groups recognize only one word, "prevention".

REFERENCES

Ad-EL, D.D., Engel hard, D., and Beer, Y. (2001). Earthquate related scald injuries – Experience from the IDF Field Hospital in Duzce, Turkey. *Journal of Burns*, **27**: 401-403.

Advanced Burn Life Support Course endorsed by the American Burn Association. Nebraska Burn Institute, 4600 Valley Road, Lincoln, Nebraska 68510

Alexander, J.W., Boyce, S.T., and Babcock, L.G. (1990). The process of microbial translocation. *Journal of Annual Surgery* **212**: 496 – 572.

Alexande r,J.W., Macmillian, B.G., and Stinneth, N.D. (1980). Beneficial effects of aggressive protein feeding in severely burned children. *Annuals of Surgery* **192**:505-507.

Allgomer, M., Burri, C., and Gruber, U.C. (1993). Toxicity of burned mouse skin in relation to burn temperature. *Journal of Surgery Forum 14:37-39*

Alonso, D., and Vabro-Gasalla, J. (1998). Burn injuries following explosion of car heaters. *Burns* **24**: 579-580.

AL – Qattan, M.M. (2000). The Friday Mass burns of the feet in Saudi Arabia. *Journal of Burns* **26**: 102-105.

Alvi, R., Walmsley, p., and James, M. I. (2001). Deep dermal burn due to contact with stomach contents – a case report. *Burns* **27**: 509-511. **161**: 209 – 212.

Amy, B.W., Mcmunus, W.F., and Goodwin, C.W. (1985). Thermal injury in the pregnant patient. *Journal of Surgery, Gynaecology and Obstetrics*

Andronicus, M., Oates, R.K., and Peat, J. (1998). Non-accidenta burns in children. *Journal of Burns* **24**: 552 – 558.

Anselmo, U.J., and Zawacka, B.E. (1987). Multispectral photographic analysis – a new quantitative tool to assist in the early diagnosis of thermal burn injury. *Annual Biomedics* **5**: 179-193.

Atkinson, R.S., Rushman, G.B., and Davies, N. (1997). Plastic surgery and burns in Lee's synopsis of anaesthesia. **11ed.** Butterwith-Heinemann Ltd, Oxford – London. 590-593.

Attalia, M.F., and AI – Bakur, A.A. (1991). Friction burns of the head caused by jogging machines - a potential hazard to children. *Burns* **17(2):** 170-171.

Arnold, E. (1993). Injury by Burning. In: The pathology of Trauma. **2ⁿᵈ ed**. Hodder and Stoughton Ltd. Great Britain. 178-191.

Aslam, A., and Khoo, C.T.K. (1997). No sense, No sensibility – A tale of two adults hair drier burns. *Burns* **23:** No. 5: 454-457.

Artz, C.P., and Yarbrough, D.R. (1992). Collagen in wound healing -thermal, chemical and electrical trauma. In: Textbook of Surgery, **9ᵗʰ ed**. Appleton-Century Crafts, New York. 85-95.

Astamian, R.D., and Lee, R.C. (1996). The physicochemical basis for thermal and non-thermal burn Injuries. *Burns* **22:** 509-519.

Averull, J.R. (1992). Anger and Aggression - An Essay on Emotion. *Springer* **30:** 23-26.

Babu, M., and Latha, B. (2001). The Involvement of free radicals in burn injury-a review. *Burns* 27: 309-317.

Baron, D.N. (2000). The kidneys. A short textbook of chemical pathology, **8ᵗʰ ed.** English Language Society, London. 171-189.

Baruchin, O., Yoffe, B., and Baruchin, A.M. (2004). Burns in in-patients by simultaneous use of cigarettes and oxygen therapy. *Burns* **30:** 836-838.

Bartle, F.J., Sun, J.H., and Wang, X.W. (1987). Burns in pregnancy. *Journal of Burn care Rehabilitation* **9:** 455-487.

Barry, A.L., Edward, M.C., and Richard, J. E. (1993). Burn Assessment. *Journal of Current practice of Surgery* **I:** 185 – 193.

Batchelor, J.S., Vanjari, S., and Budny, P. (1994). Domestic iron burns in children: A cause for concern. *Burns* **20:**(1) 74-75.

Baxter, C.R. (1994). Fluid volume and electrolyte changes of the early postburn period. *Clinical plastic surgery* **I:** 693-696.

Benmeir, P., Lusthaus, S., and Winberg, A. *et al.,* (1993). Chemical burn due to contact with soda lime on the playgrounds – a potential hazard for football players. *Burns* **19:**(4). 358-359.

Bion, J.F., Edlin, S.A., and Ramsey, G. (1983). Validation of a prognostic score in critically ill patients undergoing transport *British Medical Journal* **291:** 432-434.

Birken, G.A., and Fabri, P.G. (1981). Acute ammonia intoxication complicating multiple trauma. *Journal of Trauma* **21:** 820-822.

Blumenfeld, M., and Thompson, T.L (2000). Psychological reactions to physical illness in understanding human behaviour in health and illness. **2nd ed.** Williams and Wilkins, Baltimore. 95-107.

Boucher, J., Raglon, B., Valdez, S., and Heiffajee, A. (1990). Possible role of chemical hair care products in 10 patients with face scalp, ear, back, neck and extrimity burns. *Burns* **16:**(2). 146-147.

Brain, G.S. (1997). Burn pathophysiology -Treating mass burns in warfare disaster or terrorist strikes. *Burns* **23:** No.3. 241-242.

British Medical Association Journal (1983). The medical effects of nuclear war. Wiley. Chichester. 89-91.

Britton, K.E. (1994). Renal failure. Clinical physiology: **10th ed.** Blackwell oxford, London. 166-170.

Brokenshire, B., and Calus, F. (1984). Death from electricity. *New Zealand Medical Journal* **97:** 139.

Brown, R.J. (1999). The Day the clowns cried. History-buff. **Lttp:/www.com/library/Reffire. Ltml**.

Bull, J.P., and Lawrence, J.C. (1997). Thermal conditons which cause skin burns. *Journal of Mechanics and Electricity* **5:** 61-63.

Caplin, M. (1981). Ammonia-gas poisoning: 47 cases in a London Shelter. *Lancet* **12:** 95- 96.

Cave, B.G., Cipollon, L., and Parroni, E. (2001). A review of suicides by burning in Rome between 1947-1997 examined by the Pathology Department of the Institute of Forensic Medicine, University of Rome, 'La Sapienza'. *Burns* **27:** 227-231.

Cassell, O.O.S., and Hubble, M. (1997). Baby Walkers - still a major cause of infant burns. *Burns* **23:** No.5. 451-453.

Celikoz, B., and Senegezer, M.D. (1997). Four limb amputations due to electrical burn caused by TV antenna contact with overhead electric cable. *Burns* **23:** 81-84.

Cetinkale, O., Bele, A., Konukoglu, D., and *et a*l. (1997). Evaluation of lipid peroxidation and total antioxidant status in plasma of rats following thermal injury. *Burns* **23:** 114-116.

Cheesbrough, M. (1987). Measurement of serum bicarbonate. In: Medical laboratory manual for tropical countries. **2ⁿᵈ ed:** Vol. I. University press, Cambridge, Great Britain. 491-494.

Cheeseman, K.H. (1993). Lipid peroxidation in biological system. In: DNA and free Radicals. Ellis Horwood, London. 75-80

Chopra, I.D., and Solomon, D.H. (1994). Thyroid hormones in hepatic cirrhosis. *Journal of Clinical Endocrinology* **3:** 501-511.

Christoffel, T., and Gallagher, S.S. (1999). Injury prevention and public health. *Aspen.* 58 – 63

Christengen, J.A., Sherman, R.T., and Balis, G.A. (1980). Delayed neurologic injury secondary to high - voltage current with recovery. *Journal of Trauma* **20:** 166.

Clark, W.R., and Nieman, G.F. (2000). Smoke inhalation. *Burns* **14:** 473

Clark, W.R., Bonaventure, M., and Myers, W. (1989). Smoke inhalation and airway management at a regional Burn Unit: 1975 – 1983. Part I: Diagnosis and consequences of smoke inhalation. *Journal of Burn care and Rehabilitation 10:52.*

Clung-Chuan, L., and Annette, M.R. (2000). Landmarks in burn prevention. *Burns* **26:** 422-434.

Cocks, R. (1987). Study of 100 patients injured by London underground train, 1981 – 1986. *British medical Journal* **297:** 1527.

Cole, R.P., Shakespeare, P.G., and Chissell, H. (1991). Thermographic assessment of burns using a non-permeable membrane as wound covering. *Burns* **17:**(2). 117-122.

Cooper, M.A. (1995). Myths, Miracles and Mirages. *Sem Neurol* **15:** 358 – 361.

Cote, A.E. (1994). Field test and evaluation of residential sprinkler system. Part III. *Fire Technology* **20:** 41 – 46.

Crocq, L., and Doucet, J. (1989). Physiopathology of serious burn cases. Defence Research Group 9, Panel VIll: NATO AC/243 (Panel VIll/RSG 9) D/26.

Dannels, G.H., and Maloof, F. (1996). Regulatory mechanisms of the pituitary thyroid axis. Pathophysiology: **4ᵗʰ ed**. J.B. Lippincoth Company, Philadelphia. 341 – 344

Davies, J.W.L. (1986). Causes of major burns in two industrial areasof the United Burns: Kingdom. A survey of 3281 patients presented at the 7ᵗʰ international congress of Melbourne, Australia

Degrot, L.G., and Taurog, A. (1990). Secretion of thyroid hormones. *Journal of Endocrinology* **5:** 343 – 346.

Deitch, F A., Rightmire, D.A., and Blass, N. (1985). Management of burns in pregnant women. *Journal of Surgery, Gynaecology, Obstetrics* **16:** 1 - 4.

Department of Health, N.H.S Estates (1992). Health Guidance Note: Safe hot water and surface temperatures. London: Hmso

Diller, K.R. (1998). Modelling thermal skin burns on a personal computer. *Journal of Burn Care Rehabilation* **19:** 420-429.

Ding, Y.L., PU, S.S., Pan, Z.L., *et al*. (1987). Extensive scalds following accidental immersion in hot water pools. *Burns* **13:** 305.

Dingwall, J.A. (1983). A clinical test for differentiating second from third degree burns. *Journal of Annals of surgery* **118:** 427 – 429.

Dixion, J.J., Bird, D.A.R., and Roberts, D.V.G. (1997). Severe burns resulting from an exploding teat on a bottle of infant formula milk heated in a microwave oven. B*urns* **23:** No.3 268-269.

Dobke, M.k. (1993). Burns in children: A continued challenge. *Journal of Burn care* 65. *Rehabilatation* **14:**17-20

Donald, R.C., Pegg, S.P., and Muller, M. (1997). Self inflicted burns. *Burns* **23:** No. 6. 519 521.

Dowie, M. (1999). Pinto madness. *Mother Jones* **2:** 248-262.

Drog, E.G., Steenbergen, W., and SJO berg, F. (2001). Measurement of depth of burns by laser doppler perfusion imaging. *Burns* **27:** 561 – 568.

Dziewuiski, P. (1992). Burn wound Healing. *Burns* **8:** 269-278.

Edward, A.L. (2000). Electrical Burns. Clinics in plastic surgery: Vol. **27:** No.1. W.B. Saunders Company, Philadelphia. 133-143.

Ehrenwerth, J., Sorbo, S., and Hackel, A. (1996). Transport of critially ill adults. *Critical care medicine* **14:** 534 – 537

Eldad, A., Stern, H., Sorer, R., *et al*. (1993). The cost of an extensive burn survival. *Burns* **19:** (3). 235-238.

Eltigani, E., and Mathews, R.N. (1994). An unusual cause of sunbed burns. *Burns* **20:** (1). 87- 88.

Ermans, A.M. (1990). Endemic goiter and endemic cretinism. *Journal of Endocrinology* **3**: 501.

Essex, T.J.H., and Byrue, P.O. (1991). A laser doppler scanner for imaging blood flow in skin. *Journal Biomedical* **13**: 189.

Fathovich, G., Glustia, G., Favarato, S., *et al.* (1996). A survey of adverse events in 11241 patients with chronic viral hepatitis treated with alfa interferon. *Journal Hepatol* **24**: 38-47

Feldman, K.W., Schaller, R.Y., Feldman, J.A., *et al.* (1998). Tap water scald burns in children. *Paediatrics* **62**: 1-7.

Feller, I. (1986). What data do we need and can we survive without changing the rules? Bulletin clinical review. *Burns* **3**: 10- 14.

Fernanda, G.T., Lidia, A.R., Eneas, F., *et al.* (2000). Analysis of cost of dressings in the care of Burn patients. *Burns* **26**: 289- 90

Field, T.O., Donfinic, W., and Hansbrough, J. (1987). Beach fire burns in San Diego Country. *Burns* **13**: 416-418.

Formal, C., Goodman, C., Jacobs, B., *et al.* (1989). Burns after spinal cord injury. Archives. Physiology. *Medical Rehabilitation* **70**: 380.

Francis, B.M. (1994). Toxic substances in the environment. Wiley Ltd. New York. 75-80.

Fried, M., Kahnovitz, S., and Dagan, R. (1996). Full-thickness foot burn of a pilgrim to Mecca. *Burns* **22**: 644-645.

Fukunishi, K., Tanaka, H., Maruyama, J., *et al.* (1998) Burns in a suicide attempt related to psychiatric side effects of interferon. *Burns* **26**: 581-585.

Gabbiani, G., Hirschel, B.J., and Ryan, G.B. (1988). Granulation tissue as a contractile organ - a study of structure and function. *Journal of Experimental Medicine* **135**: 719-722.

Gamble, W.B., and Bonnecarre, E.R. (1996). Coffee, tea or frostbite? A case report inflight freezing hazard from dry ice. Aviat: *Space Environmental Medicine* **67**:880- 881.

Gong, R.K., George, A., Bang, R.I., and Lari, A.R. (2000). Liquid ammonia injury. A case report. *Burns* **26**: 409-413.

Gang, R.K., Bajee, J., and Tahboug, M. (1992). Management of thermal injury in pregnancy – An analysis of 16 patients. *Burns* **18**: 317-330.

Garcia, C., Smith, G., Cohen, D., *et al.* (1995). Electrical injuries in a paediatric emergency department. *Annals of Emergency medicine* **26**: 604.

Glasgon, J.F.T., and Graham, H.K. (1997). Burns and scalds -Management of injuries in children. **1ˢᵗ ed**. BMJ Group, BMA House, Ta vistock square, London. 113-117.

Golderg, K. (1999). The Hartford Circus fire of 1944. The concord Review. **Lttp/www.ter.Org/ circus fire. Ltml**.

Gomes, D.N., Serra, M.C.F., and Pellon, M.A. (1995). Revinter. Queima duras Rio de Janeiro, Brazil.

Goodfellow, R.C. (1985). Hydrofluoric acid burns. *British medical Journal* **290**: 937

Grant, W.M. (1984). Toxicology of the Eye: *Springfield* **11**: 8-10 Graiter, P. L., and Sniezek, J.C. (1998). Hospitalizations due to tapwater scalds. CDC Surveillnice summaries. February, MMWR Vol. **37**: 35.

Green, J.H. (1996). The Thyroid Gland. In: An introduction to human physiology. African Edition. **7ᵗʰed**. Oxford University press, Ibadan.. 162-164.

Green, M.A., and Haibach, H. (1994). Thyroid Secretion in handbook of physiology. **7ᵗʰed**. Vol.3. Williams and Wilkins, Baltimore. 135.

Green, H.N., Stoner, H. B., and Whiteby, H.J.(2001). The effect of trauma on the chemical composition of blood and tissue of man. *Clinical Science* **8**: 65-87.

Green, M.R., Allen, A., Hill, O., *et al.* (1999). The production of OH and O by stimulated human neutrophils measurements by electron paramagnetic resonance spectroscopy. *FEBS Lett* **100**: 23 – 26.

Guyton, A.C. (1996). The Thyroid hormones. In: Textbook of medical physiology: **10ᵗʰed**. W.B. Saunders company, Philadelphia. 931 – 947.

Guzin, Y.O., and Seluk, A. (2001). Thermal Injuries due to paint thinner. *Burns* **30**: 154 – 155.

Gyanog,W.F. (1998). Urea formation. Review of medical physiology: **12ᵗʰ ed.** Lange medical publications, London. 222 – 224.

Hackelt, M. E.J. (1984). The use of thermography in the assessment of depth of burn and blood supply of flaps with preliminary reports on its use in Dupuytren's contracture and treatment of varicose ulcers. *Burns* **27**: 311.

Haque, F.M., and AL-Ghazal, S. (2004). Burn from hair removal cream - A case report. *Burns* **30:** 866-867.

Hanumandass, M..L., and Voora, S.B. (1986). Acute electricity burns: A 10-Year clinical experience. *Burns* **12:** 427 – 431.

Hatton, D.V. (1979). Collagen breakdown and ammonia inhalation. *Archives of Enviromental Health* **34:** 83-87.

Hawang, J.C.F., Himel, H.N., and Edlich, F.F. (1996). Frostbite of the face after recreational misuse of nitrous oxide. *Burns* **22:** 152-153.

Heinbach, D.M., and Engrav, L.A.(1984). Burn depth estimation – man or machine. *Journal of Trauma* **24:** 373-378.

Henderson, S.O., Sotiropoulis, G., and Kila, T. (1998). Cold injury from pressurized liquid ammonia: A report of two cases. *Journal of Emegency medicine* **16:** (3). 409-412.

Henderson, P., and McConville, H. (2003). Flammable liquid burns in children. *Burns* **29:** 349-352.

Henriques, J.F., and Moritz, H.R. (1987). Studies of thermal injury: The conduction of heat to and through skin and the temperature attained therein. A theoretical and an experimental investigation. *American Journal of pathoLogy* **23:** 531 – 549.

Hennessy, J.F. (1990). Hypothyroidism: Discussion in patient management. Garden city, Medical Examination Company, New York.

Herbert, K., and Lawrence, J.C. (1989). Chemical Burns. *Burns* **15:** 381-384.

Herndon, D.N., Thompson, P.B., and Brown, M. (1987). Diagnosis, pathophysiology and treatment of inhalation injury. In: The art and science of burns care. *Aspen* **10:** 153.

HO, W.S., and Ying, S.Y. (2001). Surcidal burns in Hongkong Chinese. *Burns* **27:** 125- 127.

Horch, R., Spilker, G., and stark, G.B. (1994). Phenol burns and intoxication. *Burns* **20:** No. I. 45 – 50.

Hurren, J.S., and Dunn, K.W. (1993). Entrapment against radiators-an underestimated burn hazard to the elderly. *Burns* **19:** (6). 522-523.

Igras, E., Gahankari, D., Yuen, C., *et al.* (2003). Deep burn due to an unusual cause – boiling blood. *Burns* **29:** 287-290.

Jackson, I.T., and Macallan E.S. (1991). Plastic surgery and burns treatment. In: Morden practical nursing. Willian Hein-Mann Medical Books. London. 61-73.

Jackson, D. (1983). The Diagnosis of the depth of burning. *British Journal of Surgery* **40**: 588.

Jain, M., and Garg, A.R. (1993). Burns with pregnancy – A review of 25 cases. *Burns* **19**: (2). 166-167.

Jamal, Y.S., Ardaw, M.S. and Ashy, A.R.A.(1990). Paediatric burn injuries in the Jeddah Area of Saudi Arabia: A study of 197 patients. *Burns* **16**: No. I. 36 – 40.

James, W. (1992). Despite new regulations, caution a must when baby walkers are used. *Canada Medical Association Journal* **139**: 73.

Jelenko, C. (1984). Chemicals that burn. *Journal of Trauma* **14**: 65-72.

Jiang, S.C., Ma, N., Li, H.J., and Zhang, X.X. (2002). Effects of thermal properties and geometrical dimensions on skin burn injuries. *Burns* **28**: 713-717.

Juan, A., Ramon, P. and Santoyo, F. (2000). A rare burn injury: A case report. *Burns* **26**: 498-500.

Kagan, J.R., Nara, G.S., and Matsuda, J. (1985). Herpes simplex virus and cytomegalovirus infections in burn patients. *Journal of Trauma* **25**: 40 -45.

Kaha, A.M., Mccrady, V.C., and Rosen, V.J. (1999). Burns wound biopsy - multiple uses in patient management. *Scandivian Journal of Plastic, Reconstructive Surgery* **13**: 53.

Katcher, M.L., Landry, G.L., and Shapiro, M. (1989). Liquid-crystal thermometer use in paediatric office counseling about tap water burn presentation. *Paediatrics* **83**: 766.

Keir, J. H., Lendrum, J. and Wolman, B. (1975). Inflicted burns and scald in children. *British medical Journal* **IV**: 268.

Kemble, J.V.H., and Lamb, E.B. (1997). Electrical burns: In: Practical burns management: Hodder and Stoughton, UK. 83-87.

Kemble, J.V.H., and Lamb, E.B. (1997). Aetiology, incidence and mortality of burns: In: Practical burns management. Hodder and Stoughton, UK. 4 – 8.

Kloppenberg, F.W.H. and Beerthuizen, G.I.D. (2001). Perfusion of burn wounds assessed by laser doppler imaging is related to burn depth and healing time.
Burns: 27:359 – 363 Elsevier Science Ltd and ISBI. Great Britain.pp 359 – 363.

Koller, J. (1991). High tension electrical arc-induced thermal burns caused by railway overhead cables. Burns 17: 412.

Kumar, P., and Thomas, C.P. (2001). High-tension electrical injury from a telephone receiver. A case report. *Burns* **27:** 502 -503.

Kumar, P., Chirayil, P.T. (1999). Vapour injury: A case report. *Burns* **25:** 265 – 268.

Lnwrence, J.C., and Bull, J.P. (1986). Thermal conditions which cause skin burns. *Journal of Instrument mechanics* **5:** 6.

Lawrence, J.C. (1996). Burns and scalds: aetiology and prevention. In: Principles and practice of burns management. Churchill Livingstone, London. 105-108.

Leduc, D., Gris, P., and Lhenrenx, P. (1992). Acute and long term respiratory damage following inhalation of ammonia. *Thorax* **47:** 755 – 757.

Lee, R.C. (1992). Electrical trauma. Cambridge press, U.K. 102- 107

Levine, M.S. (1987). Fire victims: medical outcomes and demographic characteristics. *American Journal of Public Health* **67:** 1077.

Linares, A. Z., and Linares, H.A.(1990). Burn prevention: the need for a comprehensive approach. *Burns* **16:** 281-285.

Lindsey, T.A.R. (1992). Assessment of thermal burns: critical care of the burned patient: **1st ed.** Cambridge University press, NewYork, USA. 15 – 31.

Lindsey, T.A.R. (1992). Inhalation injury: critical care of the burned patient: **1st ed.** Cambridge University press, New York, USA. 59-76.

Lopez, R.E., and Holle, A. (1995). Demography of lightning casualties. *Neurology* **15:** 286 – 296.

Lofts, J.A. (1991). Cost analysis of a major burn. *New Zealand Medical Journal* **16:** (4) 488 – 490

Luce, E.A. (1990). Electrical injury. *Journal of Plastic Surgery* **12:** 514.

Luce, E.A., and Dowden, W.L. (1990). High - tension electrical injury of the upper extremity. *Journal of Surgery Gynaecology and Obstetrics* **38:** 47.

Macdonald, R.C., Banks, J.G., and Led, J. (1981). Transport of the injured. *Injury* **12:** 225 – 235.

Manktelow, A. (1990). Burn injury and management in Liberia. *Burns* **16:** (6). 432-436.

Marktelow, A., Meyer, A.A., Herzog, S.R., *et al.*(1989). Analysis of lifeexpectancy and living status of elderly patients surviving a burn injury. *Journal of Trauma* **29:** 203-207.

Marano, M.A., and Fong, Y. (1990). Serum cachectin/tumour necrosis factor in critically ill patients with burns correlates with infection and mortality. *Journal of Surgery Gynaecology Obstetrics* **170:** 32-35.

Marchesan, W.G., and Ferreira, F. (1997). Suicide attempted by burning in Brazil. *Burns* **23:** No. 3. 270 – 271.

Martin, D.W., Mayes, P.H., and Rodwell, V. (1996). The thyroid. In: Harpers review of biochemistry: **24thed**. Lange medical Ltd, California. 468 – 472.

Mcclung, M.R., and Greer, M.A. (1980). Treatment of hyperthyroidism. *Annual Review of Medicine* **31:** 385-390.

Mcgowan, G.K. (1985). The laboratory assessment of thyroid function. *Journal of Clinical Pathology* **28:** 206-254.

Mccord, J.M. (1993). The superoxide free radical: Its biochemistry and pathophysiology. *Surgery* **94:** 412 – 415.

Mckenzie, J.M., and Zakarija, M. (1989). Hyperthyroidism. *Endocrinology* **10:** 429-433.

Mellor, S.G., Rice, P., and Cooper, G.J. (1991). Vesicant burns. *British Journal of Plastic Surgery* **6:** 434-432.

Michael, M., Marcot, M., and Scoeps, T. (1993). Reactions: In: Psychological care of the burn and trauma patient: **2nded.** Wilkins and Willians, USA. 95-104

Miilea, T.P., Kukan, J.O., and Smooth, M.(1989). Anhydrous ammonia injuries. *Journal of Burn Care Rehabilitation* **10:** (5).448 – 453.

Moghtader, J., Homel, H., and Demun, E. (1993). Electrical burn injuries of workers using portable Aluminum ladder near overhead power lines. *Burns* **19:** 441 – 443.

Moritz, A.R., and Henriques, F.C.(1987). Studies of thermal injury: the relative importance of time and surface temperature in the causation of cutaneous burns. *American Journal of Pathology* **23:** 695-720.

Moritz, H.R., Henriques, F., and Melan, R.(1984). The effects of inhaled heat on the air passage and lungs: anexperimental investigation. *American Journal of Pathology* **21:** 311 – 331.

Muir, I.F.K., Barclay, T.L., and Settle, J. (1983). The scope of the burn problem: In: Burns and their treatment: **3rd ed.** 1 - 13.

Muir, I.F.K., Barclay, T.L., and Settle, J. (1987). Local treatment of the wound: In: Burns and their treatment: **3rded**: Butterworth and Co. Ltd. Great Britain. 55-70.

Muir, I.F.K., Barclay, T.L., and Settle, J. (1987). Scars and contractures: In: Burns and their treatment:3rded.

Munster, A.M Butterworth of Co. Ltd. Great Britain. 350-354.., and Smith, M.M.(1993). Translocation-incidentalphenomenon or true pathology?. *Annals of Surgery* **218:** 321 – 325.

Mustard, J.C. (1991). The treatment of burns in infancy and childhood. *Journal of Plastic Surgery* **12:** 531-560.

Muchiberger, T., Vogt, P.M., and Munster, A. (2001). The long- term consequences of lightning injuries. *Burns* **27:** 829-833.

Murray, J.P. (1988). A study of the prevention of hot tap water burns. *Burns* **14:** 185-190.

Naqui, Z., Enoch, S., and Shah, M. (2005). Glass front of gas fire places: a clear and present danger. *Burns* **29:** 349-352.

Niazi, Z. B.M., Tssex, T.S.H. and Papini, R. (1993). A new laser doppler scanner, a valuable adjunct in burn depth assessment. *Burns* **19:** (6). 485-489.

Nightwear (safety) Regulations. (1985). No. 2043 HMSO, U.K.

Nightwear and Fire. (1985). A guide to the nightwear regulations. Consumer safety unit. Department of Trade and Industry, U.K.

NHS Estate Health Guidance Note. (1992). Safe hotwater and surface temperatures. ISBN O11 321404 9. HMSO London.

Ohashi, M., Kitagawa, N., and Ishikwa, T. (1986). Lighting injurycaused by discharges accompanying flashovers: a clinical and experimental study of death and survival. *Burns* **12:** 496-501

Onuba, O., and Udoidiok, E. (1987). The problems and prevention of burns in developing countries. *Burns* **13:** 382.

Oluwasanmi, J.O. (1979). Burns: Plastic surgery in the tropics introduction for medical students and surgeons: **1st ed.** 45-79.

Oslen, E.A. (1999). Methods of hair removal. *American Journal of Dermatology* **40:** (2). 143- 155.

Ostrow, L.B., Bongard, F.S., Sacks, S.T., *et al.* (1985). Major burns resulting from scalds: The california burn registry experience. *Journal of Burn Care Rehabilitation* **6:** 350.

Oughterson, A.W., and Warren, S. (1986). Medical effects of the atomic bomb in Japan. Mcgraw Hill, New York.

Papaevangelou, J., Batchelor, J.S., and Roberts, A. A.N. (1995). Motor vehicle related burns: a review of 107 cases. *Burns* **21:** 36-38.

Pegg, S.P., and Seawright, A.A. (1993). Burns due to cooking oils. *Burns* **9:** 362.

Pfister, R.R. (1983). Chemical injuries of the eye. *Opthalmology***90:** 1246.

Phillips, A.W., and Cope, O. (1980). Burn therapy. *Annals of Surgery* **152:** 762.

Pruitt, B.A., and Mason, A.D.J. (1992). Electric shock and lightning: Vol. I. **2ⁿᵈ ed**. 126.

Purdue, G., Hunt, J., and Prescott, P. (1988). Child abuse by burning an index of suspicion. *Journal of Trauma* **28:** 221-224.

Rabban, J., Adler, J., Rosen, C., *et al.* (1997). Electrical injury from subway third rails: serious injury associated with intermediate voltage contact. *Burns* **23:** No.6. 515-518.

Rainsford, M. (1987). Forward: Burns and their treatment. **3ʳᵈ ed**. Butterworth & Co. Ltd. London. i-ii.

Rainsay, I. (1986). Diseases of the thyroid: In: a synopsis of endocrinology and metabolism: **3ʳᵈ ed**. Techno House, Red cliffe way, England. 36 – 73.

Read, A.E., Burrith, D.W., and Heiver, R.L. (1986). Thyroid gland: In: Mordern medicine: 3ʳᵈ ed. 194-212. English Language Book society Churchill livingstone, Great Britain. 194-212.

Renz, B.M., and Sherman, R. (1992). Automobile carburetor and radiator-related burns. *Journal of Burn Care Rehabilitation* **13:** 414 -421.

Renz, M.R., and Sherman, R. (1994). Hot tar burns: Twenty-seven hospitalized cases. *Journal of Burn care Rehabilitation* **15:** 341 –345.

Robbins, J., Bondy, P.K., and Rosenberg, L.t. (1995). Metabolic control and diseases. 8ᵗʰ ed. W.B. Saunders co. Philadethia. 1325.

Robson, M.C., and Kicaw, J.O. (1991). The burn wound. *Journal of Top Emergency Medical* **3**: 56 - 60.

Rom, W.N. (1992). Environment and occupational medicine. **2ⁿᵈ ed**. Little Brown & Co., Boston. 529-530.

Roscoe, M.H. (1983). Clinical significance of creatinine. *Journal of Clinical Pathology* **6**: 207-209.

Rozenbaum, D., Baruchin, A.M., and Dafaa, Z. (1991). Chemical burns of the eye with special reference to alkali burns. *Burns* **17**: (2). 136 – 140.

Ryan, C.A., Shankowasky, H.R., and Tredget, E.E. (1992). Profile of the paediantric burn patient in a canadian burn centre. *Burns* **18**: No. 4. 262 – 272.

Ryan, F., Longenecker, C.G., and Vincent, R.W. (1982). Effects of pregnancy on healing of burns. *Surgery Forum* **13**: 483.

Sagi, A.A., Baruchir, A.M. and Schraf, S. (1997). HOT betumen burns: 92 hospitalied patients. *Burns* **23**: No. 5. 438 -441.

Saffle, J.R. (1993). The 1942 fire at Boston's cocoanut grove nightclub. *American Journal of Surgery* **166**: 581-591.

Salisbury, R.E. (1990). Thermal burns in plastic surgery. Plastic Surgery: Vol. 1. W.B. Saunders Co, Philadelphia. 787-813

Sarhadi, N.S., Murray, G.D., Reid, W.H. (1995). Burn trends in Scotland. *Burns* **21**: 612- 615.

Sengezer, M., Damar, H., and Selman, N. (1985). Electrical burn caused by contact of radio receiver antenna with overhead cable. *Burns* **21**: 467 – 468.

Settle, J.A.D., Muir, I.F.K., and Barclay, T.L. (1987). Burns of special types. In: Burns and their treatment: **3ʳᵈ ed**. Butterworth and Co. Ltd, Great Britain. 137.

Settle, J.A.D., Muir I.F.K., and Barclay, T.L. (1987). Local treatment of the burn wound: In: Burns and their treatment. **3ʳᵈ ed**. Butterworth and Co. Ltd, Great Britain. 55-59.

Shaw, J.M., and Robson, M.C. (1996). Electrical injuries. Total burn care: **2ⁿᵈ ed**. W.B. Saunders, Philadelphia. 401-410

Shiyanik, L., Mcmanul, A.T., and Vanglan G. (1996). Effects of environment on infection in burn patients. *Archives of Surgery* **121**: 31 – 33.

Sharpe, D.T., Roberts, A. H., and Burdey, T.L. (1985). Treatment of burns casualties. After fire at Bradford city football club ground. *British Medical Journal* **291**: 945-949.

Singh, S.P., Santosh, P.J., and Arasthi, P. (1998). A psychosocial study of self- immolation in India. *Scandinivian Acta Psychiatry* **97**: 71 – 75.

Sparkes, B.G. (1997). In warfare, disaster or terrorisk strikes. *Burns* **23**: (3) 238-247.

Spurr, A.D., and Shakespare, P.G. (1996). Incidence of hypertrophic scarring in burned and injured children. *Burns* **16**: 179-181.

Smith, A.C., Barclay, A., and Quaba, K. (1997). The bigger the burn, the greater the stress. *Burns* **23**: No. 4. 291-294.

Solem, L., Fisher, R., and Strate, R.G. (1997). The natural history of electrical injury. *Journal of Trauma* **17**: 487 – 491.

Sotiroponlos, G., Kila, T., and Gougherty, W. (1998). Cold injury from pressurized ammonia: A report of two cases. *Journal of Emergency Medicine* **16**: 409 - 412.

Staley, M., Richard, R., and Warden, G.D. (1996). Functional outcomes for the patients with burn injuries. *Journal of Burn Care Rehabilitation* **17**: (4). 362 – 370.

Stanbury, J.B. (1980). Endemic goitre and endemic cretinism: **3rd ed**. Wiley & Sons, New York, U.S.A. 60-65.

Sterling, K. (1981). The importance of circulating triiodothyronine. *New England Journal of Medicine* **284**: 271.

Stern, M.B. (1985). In vivo evaluation of microcirculation bycoherent light scattering. *Nature* **254**: 56 – 58.

Sternick, I., Gomes, R.D., and Serra, M. (2000). "Train Surfers": analysis of 23 cases of electrical burns caused by high tension railway Overhead cables. *Burns* **26**: 470 – 473.

Still, J., Orlet, H., and Law, E. (1997). Electrocution due to contact of industrial equipment with power lines. *Burns* **23**: No. 7/8. 573 – 575.

Still, J.M., Law, E.G., and Klavuhu, K.C. (2001). Diagnosis of burn depth using laser- induced indocianine green fluorescence: a preliminary clinical trial. *Burns* **27**: 364-371.

Stoffman, J.M., Bass, M.G., and Fox, A.M. (1984). Head injuries related to the use of baby walkers. *Journal of Canada Medical Association* **131**: 573-575.

Stone, M., Ahmed, J., and Evans, I. (2000). The Continuing risk of domestic hot water scalds in the elderly. *Burns* **26:** 347-350.

Summerlin, W.T., Walder, A.L., and Moncrief, J. (1987). White phosphorus burns and massive haemolysis. *Journal of Trauma* **21:** 476.

Suliman, M.T. (2004). Congenital burns. *Burns* **30:** 197-198.

Sydney, S.G., Jeffrey, S., and Greenspon, F. (2001). Management of burns injuries during pregnancy. *Burns* **27:** 394-397.

Takagi, S. (1995). Psychiatric manifestations of interferon therapy: *Seishin Igatu* **37:** 344 – 358.

Teodorczyk, J., Sparkes, B.G., Mills, G., *et al.* (1991). Immuno suppression follows systemic T - lymphocyte activation in burns patient. *Clinical Immunology* **85:** 575 517.

Teplitz, C., David, D., and Mason, A.D. (1984). Pseudomonas burn wound sepsis. *Journal of Surgery Review* **4:** 200 – 202.

Tejerina, C., Reig, A., and Codina, J. (1992). Burns in patients over 60 years old: epidemiology and mortality. *Burns* **18:** No.2. 109 -112.

Thompson, R.M., and Carrougher, G. (1998). Burn prevention. *Journal of Burn Care and Therapy* **8:** 497–512.

Thompson, J.A. (1994). Clinical tests of thyroid function: **4th ed.** crosby lockwood staples, London. 1 - 8.

Tietz, N.W. (2000). Thyroid function: In: fundamentals of clinical chemistry: **8th ed**. W.B. Saunders Co, Philadelphia 824-847.

Tietz, N.W. (2000). Determination of serum creatunine. fundamentals of clinical chemistry: **8th ed**. W.B. Saunders Co, Philadelphia. 994 -998.

Tietz, N.W. (2000). Chloride determination. In: fundamentals of clinical chemistry: **8th ed**. W.B. Saunders Co, Philadelphia. 880 – 882.

Till, G.O., Guilds, L.S., and Mahrougui, M. (1989). Role of xanthine oxidase in thermal injury of skin. *American Journal of Pathology* **13:** 195.

Tiwari, V.K., and Sharma, D. (1999). Kite flying: a unique but dangerous mode of electrical injury in children. *Burns* **25:** 537 - 539.

Traber, D.L., and Herndon, D.N. (1990). Pathophysiology of smoke inhalation: In: smoke inhalation and burns. mcgraw hill incorporated, NewYork. 61.

UK Night wear (Safety) Regulation (1985). SI 1985/2043.243. Ullmann, Y., Blumerfeld, Z. Hakim, M., and *et al*. (1997). Urgent delivery, the treatment of choice in term pregnant Women with extended burn injury. *Burns* **23**: No.2. 157-159.

Uman, M.A., and Krider, E.P. (1989). Natural and artificially initiated lightning. *Science* **246**: 457 – 464.

US Product safety Commission (1995). Directorate for epidemiology. National injury information clearing House, Bethesda. Report period 1993 – 1995.

US Department of Health and Human Resources / Public Health Service. (1989). Injuries associated with UItraviolet tanning devices – Wisconsin. morbed motality week Report **38**: 333.

US Fire Administration. (1983). Residential smoke and fire detector coverage in the United states. Findings from a 1982 survey: federal emergency management agency, Washington D.C.

US consumer product safety commission. (1999). Fireworks. CPSC document. No. 12.

Utiger, R.D.(1999). Hypothyroidism. *Journal of Endocrinology* **12**: 491.

Voley, H., Gowenlock, A., and Bell,M.(1990). Chloride determination: In: practical clinical biochemistry: **7th ed**. university press, cambridge, Great Britain. 786 – 790.

Virendra, K. (2003). Burnt wives – a study of suicides. *Burns* **29**: 31-35

Wallace, A.B. (1999). Historical note. *Burns* **25**: 3 – 5.

Walmsley, R.N., and Guerin, G.H. (1993). Electrolyte disorders. A guide to diagnostic clinical chemistry: **4th ed**. Blackwell company, London. 87-90.

Walker, A.R. (1990). Fatal tapwater scald burns in the USA, 1979-1986. *Burns* **16**: 49-52.

Ward Platt, M.P., Anand, K.J., and Aynsley, A. (1989). The ontogeny of the metabolic and endocrine stress response in human foetus, neonate and child. *Intensive Care Medicine* **15**: 544 – 545.

Watts, A.M., Tyler, M.P., Perry, M., and *et al*. (2001). Burn depth and its histological measurements. *Burns* **27**: 154 – 160.

Wetli, C.V. (1996). Keraunopathology: an analysis of 45 fatalities. *American Journal of Forensic Medicine Pathology* **17**: 89 – 98.

Whitby, L.G., Percy - Robb, I.W., and Smith, A. (2000). Thyroid hormones: In: lecture notes on clinical chemistry, **5ᵗʰ ed**. Blackwell scientific publication, London. 322-342.

W.H.O. Lab/86.3 (1986). Methods recommended for essential clinical chemistry and haematological tests for intermediate hospital Labs. 95 – 97, 114-117

Willems, J.L. (1989). Clinical management of mustard gas casualties. *Annales Mediciniae Belgicare* **3:** supplement. 89-96.

Wilson, D. I., and Barlic, F.B. (1999). Night attire burns in young girls - the return of an old adversary. *Burns* **25:** 269 – 271.

Wisdom, G.B. (1996). Enzyme immunoassay. *Journal of Clinical Chemistry* **22:** 1243 – 1246.

WWW. en. wikipedia. org. Heat shock protein.

WWW. antigenics.com. Heat shock protein: Basics.

Wyllie, F.J., and Sutherland, A.B. (1991). Measurement of surface temperature as an aid to the diagnosis of burns depth. *Burns* **17:** (2). 123 – 128.

Yarbrough, D.R. (1998). Burns due to aerosol can explosion. *Burns* **24:** 270-271

Ying, S.Y., and HO, W.S. (2001). Playing with fire - a significant cause of burn injury in children. *Burns* **27:** 39-41.

Zikria, R.A. (1982). Smoke and carbon monoxide poisoning. *Journal of Trauma* **12:** 641

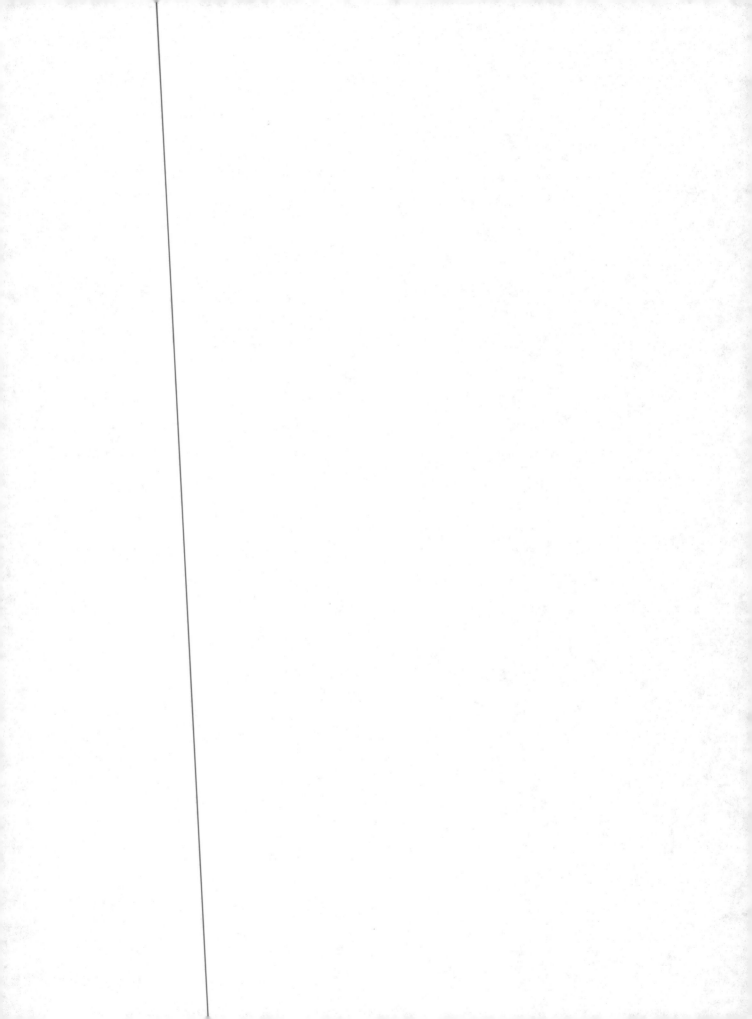

Printed in the United States
By Bookmasters